A HISTORY OF THE DEVELOPMENT OF JAPANESE THOUGHT
from A.D. 592 to 1868

by

NAKAMURA Hajime

Volume II

KOKUSAI BUNKA SHINKOKAI
(Japan Cultural Society)
Tokyo, 1969

First edition, 1967
Second edition, 1969

Published by KOKUSAI BUNKA SHINKOKAI, 1-1-18, *Shirokanedai, Minato-ku, Tokyo (108), Japan. Distributed by* JAPAN PUBLICATIONS TRADING COMPANY, LTD., *P.O. Box 5030 Tokyo International, Tokyo, Japan; 1255 Howard Street, San Francisco, California 94103; 175 Fifth Avenue, New York, New York 10010. Copyright* © *1967 by Kokusai Bunka Shinkokai; all rights reserved. Printed in Japan by* GENERAL PRINTING CO., LTD., YOKOHAMA.

LCC Card No. 74-97242

If America is called a "melting pot" of different culture, Japan may be the one, too, of sundry currents of religions and philosophy. Even in the pre-Nara period, strong influences of Chinese and Indian thoughts are quite evident. In the middle age of the warriors' regime, Zen Buddhism comes across the sea over to Japan. Then by the visit of Jesuits in the 16th century European Catholic impact led to great religious and political discussions and it ended up by the civil war of Kirishitan. Even during the closed door policy of the Tokugawa shogunate, Chinese philosophies were imported and translated into Japanese philosophy. The tendency became more dynamic once the country was open to the Western countries in 1868. It reached to a stage that Dr. Reischauer called Japan with her westernized modern attire as a part of the Far West, instead of Far East.

It may be an interesting question to ask whether there existed or exists any Japanese thought of its own. The question was already raised by such scholars or philologists of the Tokugawa period as KEICHU, KADANO Azumamaro, MOTOORI Norinaga and HIRATA Atsutane who created a school of Kokugaku or National Study which unfortunately came to be one of the guiding principles of nationalistic movement of the late Tokugawa and early Meiji thinkers and politicians.

The author of this book is Professor of Hindu Philosophy and Dean of the Literature Department at the University of Tokyo. He opened a new horizon of comparative study of Asian thought when he wrote his *The Ways of Thinking of Eastern Peoples: India-Tibet-Japan* (English edition, 1964).

This book is a compilation of the various articles the author has written in different occasions on Japanese thought. There are some repetitious phrases in chapters. But time being limited it was impossible to reedit them entirely. Some revision should be undertaken in later days.

March 1967

Kokusai Bunka Shinkokai

A number of excellent Western works have already been published on the history of Japanese philosophy. One thinks, for example, of the late TSUCHIDA Kyōson's *Contemporary Thought of Japan and China* (London: Williams and Norgate Ltd.), which appeared about forty years ago, and of Father Gino K. PIOVESANA's *Recent Japanese Philosophical Thought, 1862–1962: A Survey* (Tokyo: Enderle Bookstore), published in 1963. Others might also be mentioned. Of all of them, however, it must be noted that they understand Japanese philosophy to have started with the Meiji Restoration and with the entrance of Western culture into Japan. My point of view, however, is fundamentally different, for I am of the opinion that even prior to the Meiji Restoration there was a long history of philosophy in Japan.

If compared with Greece, India, or China, Japanese philosophy got a late start, but if compared with the various countries of Europe, it was not far behind. The present book is an attempt to trace, in historical perspective, the problems considered in the history of philosophy in Japan.

My particular field of interest is the study of Indian thought, and it is only occasionally, as time permits, that I undertake a study of Japanese Buddhism. But as I am interested in comparative philosophy, and believe that it will become increasingly important in future, I have allowed myself the liberty of writing this brief account of philosophy in pre-modern Japan. Readers of this account will discover, I believe, that Japanese philosophers grappled with the same kinds of problems as did philosophers in the West, in India, and in China, and that the history of Japanese philosophical thought follows much the same course of development as that found elsewhere.

This book was written at the request of the Kokusai Bunka Shinkokai. Due to space limitations and time deadlines, a more detailed description could not be given. I hope to write a fuller account at another time.

The greater part of the book I wrote originally in English. Chapter IV, however, on the "Controversy between Buddhism and Christianity," and Chapter VI, on "Modern Trends—Specific Problems of the Tokugawa Period," were translated by Mr. ABE Yoshiya and Father William JOHNSTON in proportions indicated in the text.

To all these people I want to take this opportunity to express my profound gratitude.

NAKAMURA Hajime

March 1967

Editorial Notes

1. Romanization: The Hepburn system with minor modifications has been employed in the romanizations of Japanese words.
2. Personal names: In accordance with the Japanese practice, the family names precede the given names.

CHAPTER V

MODERN TRENDS—General Features of the Tokugawa Period

1. Introductory Remarks

People often say that Eastern countries had nothing which could properly be termed a modern age before the introduction of Western civilization. They say that there had not yet appeared what might be called "modern" ways of thinking.

This appears at first glance to be true, but if we investigate the history of modern Eastern thought more thoroughly, we come to see the gradual indigenous development of modern conceptions of man and ethical values, corresponding to, yet different from, those in the modern West.

In the following, I propose to discuss some features of the thought in Japan of the Tokugawa period, of nearly the same period as the modern West.

Generally speaking, it might be said that many religious sects have remained as medieval, in their behavior as in their manner of valuation in the Tokugawa period also. What then do we mean by medieval ways of valuation? They are generally characterized by the following features:

(1) The absolute authority of traditional religions was admitted by the people in general who were under their strict control. Traditional symbols were stereotyped for a long period.

(2) Consequently, religious orders were extremely influential in the realm of social relations.

(3) The absolute sacredness of religious canons was stressed. Scholarship was no more than deduction from, and the elucidation of, the fundamental dogmas of religions. Learning was, in the main, scholastic.

Free thinking was not permitted; heretics were punished, scepticism was abhorred.

(4) The tendency of thought was, generally speaking, other-worldly. Religious life was regarded as noble, secular life as vile and mean.

(5) As for social structure, a feudalistic hierarchy of status was accepted by the common people, and was enforced by authority.

(6) Cultural life was limited to the upper classes; common people hardly participated in it.

Such ways of thinking and behavior were characteristic of the medieval West and Japan. And if we assume that modern ways of thinking involve the casting off of these, it is necessary that we should investigate Japanese thought from the same viewpoint as Western thought, although we should not overlook the difference which exists between them.

The literature written in this period is voluminous. However, focusing our investigation, we want to point out and discuss some conspicuous features in the change of thought which can be found in the works of some Japanese thinkers of the past during the four or five centuries before the introduction of Western civilization at the Meiji Restoration.

These features could be found only in their incipient stage, and were not influential enough to change the whole society. But we should not overlook them. They are worth notice.

As the motivating power we shall first mention and discuss the critical attitude.

2. Critical Attitude

Consciousness of Ego

It is said that modern thought began with the consciousness of the self (*cogito ergo sum*). The attitude of esteeming man as such makes one aware of the problem of *ego*.

In Japanese Buddhism the process of the appearance of ego-consciousness can be noticed. Master T'ien-t'ai (538–597), the founder of the Chinese T'ien-t'ai school, declared that one should not entertain doubt towards one's own master. This way [1]of thinking was most conspicuous in later Zen Buddhism, which esteems transmission from master to disciple. But in modern Japan the opposite attitude was expressed. "To be honest one must declare one's own doubts, if he has any, as I do." [2]

Even in Zen Buddhism a critical attitude was expressed towards the founder. To illustrate: Dōgen (1200–1253) denounced the theory of 'perceiving one's own nature intuitively' set forth in the Sūtra of the Sixth Patriarch. But Tenkei (1648–1735), his spiritual descendant, rejected Dōgen's opinion as 'absurd sheer nonsense.'[3] According to the traditional attitude, "one's own enlightenment should be conveyed face to face, from master to disciple, and it should be approved by a single master." It is likely that this attitude reflected the feudalistic tendency of the Tokugawa period. But Tenkei gave a different interpretation. In this phrase "master" means 'one's own self'; "disciple" also means 'one's self'; "a single master" means 'one's self.' So, the whole phrase means 'the attainment of one's own or true self by oneself.' We need not practice under the guidance of a single teacher. Even by looking at peach blossoms one can make one's own self clear.[4]

But the Japanese ego-consciousness was greatly different from the Western one of the same period. In Zen Buddhism it was supposed that the true spirit of religion should be handed down from master to disciple. According to the Western way of understanding, the self of the master must be something different from that of the disciple. But Tenkei asserts that both are one; i.e., essentially the transmission of the spirit of religion is done from the Great Self to the Great Self. "The transmission of the Self cannot be caused by others. It is the transmission from one's self to one's self."[5] Master Dōgen taught 'learning one's self,' and Tenkei explained that it was nothing but the way of following 'the Great Self.' 'To learn (know) one's self' was interpreted as meaning 'to know one's Mind.' 'To know one's Mind' was emphasized by such Zen priests as Munan (1603–1676), Bankei, etc. ISHIDA Baigan (1685–1748) also said: "To know Mind is said to be the beginning of learning (science)."[6] It was said that it should be found out by oneself.

As the Japanese concept of the self differs from the Western one, its

ethical implication became different. In the West individualism was regarded as the basis of ethics. But in Japan the removal of conflict between different individuals was regarded as the ethical ideal. This was
probably due to Buddhist influence, but even among non-Buddhists
this thought is noticed. ISHIDA Baigan, the founder of the *Shingaku*
school, said as follows: "Real learning consists in attaining complete
freedom from the personal Mind." "You must conceive this selflessness as
a Law."[7] Among the thinkers of the modern West egoism and individualism were clearly distinguished; but among the Japanese thinkers of the
same period this distinction was not so clearly made. Instead, another
way of approach to the self was displayed. Hakuin's (1636–1769) Introspection was a kind of autosuggestion based on the idea that man's body
and spirit form a close unity. This method of Introspection through
which man, in a certain sense, finds his true self, liberates spiritual forces
which greatly influence also man's bodily well-being.[8] However, the
thinkers who advocated the significance of the individual were not entirely lacking. For example, NINOMIYA Sontoku (1787–1856) valued the
individual in a way that was unusual for his time. Once, pointing to the
statue of the Buddha that represents him as saying when he was born,
"Between heaven and earth only I am holy," Sontoku said to his disciples: "The Buddha did not use those words out of false pride, nor must
they be applied exclusively to him. The teaching ought to be that every
man thinking of himself should feel, that between heaven and earth
there is no more noble man than he, for were he not existent there would
be nothing."[9] Originally this legend came into existence in order to
glorify the superhuman quality of the Buddha among later devout Buddhists.[10] Sontoku's interpretation seems to have been a slightly modernized one. But here we find the assertion of the dignity and significance
of the individual in its incipient stage.

   The consciousness of ego and the critical spirit finally led to the appearance of some materialists. In the modern West materialism occurred:
BACON and HOBBES, in England, and La METREE, D'OLBACH, DIDEROT,
etc., were its advocates before MARX and ENGELS. With regard to the
Japanese counterparts, as those who prepared the way for materialism

we can mention KAIBARA Ekken (1630–1714), OGYŪ Sorai (1666–1728), DAZAI Shuntai (1680–1747), TOMINAGA Nakamoto (1715–1746), MIURA Baien (1723–1789), MINAKAWA Kien (1731–1804), and those who approached materialism KAMADA Ryūkō (1733–1821), YAMAGATA Bantō (1746–1821) and ANDŌ Shōeki (1707–c. 1760), although Japan prior to the Meiji Restoration may be said to have had no materialists in the strict sense of the word.[11] They were anti-religious, but their thoughts were limited to a small circle, and they left little influence. It was only due to the efforts of some foreign scholars such as the late E. H. NORMAN[12] and a Russian communist scholar that Japanese intellectuals in general came to notice the existence of materialists in the late feudal days.

Empirical Inquiry

In the West the modern age began with critical inquiry by means of doubt. Doubt was encouraged in China as in the West.

In the West doubts were first directed towards miracles which were essential to the faith of the Medieval Ages. In Japan also we can trace a similar movement. Miracles were already repudiated in the Medieval Ages by Master Dōgen who said: "People commonly believe that occult powers of Buddhas are such as exhaling water and fire from the body of inhaling water from the ocean into the pores of body." These may be called "small occult powers," but they are not worthy of the name of the true occult powers. The true occult powers, that is to say, "great occult powers," exist within and only within the simple everyday occurrences of "drinking tea, eating rice, drawing water, and carrying faggots." This is the "occult power of Buddha" or "the occult power of one who aspires to be a Buddha." One who practices this power will eventually become "an occult-power Buddha." It means that the true miracle is the fact that one lives righteously one's own daily life.[13] SUZUKI Shōsan (1579–1655) repudiated miracles set forth by Catholicism. He said: "There should be no miracle in the true religion. In Japan the chief miracle workers are foxes and badgers."[14] YOSHIDA Shōin (1830–1859), the nationalist leader, strongly criticized the miracle stories mentioned in the Kannon Sūtra.[15] But in Japan the problem of miracles did not cause much trouble, because miracles were not regarded as essential to Buddhism.

NINOMIYA Sontoku said that the true teaching should be read from the unwritten sacred book of nature. He had a poem: "Without sound, without odor, heaven and earth repeat over and over again the unwritten sacred book." If you wish to read this book you must close your physical eyes and open your spiritual eyes. He says there are mistakes in the written books and therefore he compares them with the unwritten book of nature and unless they are in harmony with the universe-book he rejects them.[16]

His sole reliance upon experience led him to practical attitude. NINOMIYA said: "True learning does not consist in knowledge of books; it must be practical and capable of practical application."[17] The idea of "practical learning (jitsugaku)" was espoused not only by SATŌ Nobuhiro (1769–1850) and others, but also by such a novelist as TAKIZAWA Bakin (1767–1848).[18]

In Japan some ingenious intellectuals engaged in scientific researches and inventions. For example, the activities of HIRAGA Gennai (1728–1779) have many similarities to those of Benjamin FRANKLIN in his experiments with electricity, etc. But their attempts did not develop.

Nature and Natural Law

The concept of a "natural order" had become widespread in seventeenth and eighteenth century Europe. Corresponding to it in Japan of nearly the same period the concept of natural law was advocated by many thinkers.

Universality of truth came to be stressed. Master Munan said: "CONFUCIUS said: 'My doctrine is that of an all-pervading unity.'[19] The purport of this saying is (the Way's) pervading Heaven and Earth. It is tantamount to the Buddhist Great Wisdom (Maha-prajñā)."[20] Whether such an interpretation of the Great Wisdom is right or not is in need of further examining. But Munan took it for asserting universality of truth. Such an opinion was conspicuous among liberal Zen priests and Shingaku teachers and scholars of a new tendency, such as Jiun Sonja (1718–1804) in the Tokugawa period, etc.

St. Jiun, the pioneer of Sanskrit scholarship in Japan, stressed the idea with a rationalistic attitude. "In this world there are the true Laws which benefits it always. Those who have open eyes can see these Laws as clearly as they see the sun and the moon. Whether a Buddha appears or whether a Buddha does not appear, (regardless of it) this world exists, and human beings exist. These Ten Virtues will always be manifest along them (i.e., so long as they exist)."[21]

Here we are surprised by the striking similarity of the concepts of natural law between GROTIUS and Jiun. However, GROTIUS was a Westerner. He says: "And yet God may be called the author of natural law, since He is the author of Nature, and therefore wills this law to be valid." Jiun's opinion is quite different. According to him, nature and law are nothing but Buddha himself.

Jiun found the essence of Buddhism in observing natural law, which could be termed as the observance of the Ten Virtues. "It is true of only the teachings of the Ten Virtues that they never change. Throughout all the ages, both ancient and modern, and throughout all lands they constitute the suitable and true Path for both the wise and the ignorant, the superior man and the inferior man, and for both men and women."[22]

Formerly, and even after the introduction of Western civilization in the Meiji era, Shintoism was regarded as the principle or rallying point of jingoistic nationalism. However, St. Jiun explained away Shintoism as the universal way of all mankind. What he called Shinto may be summed up in a word by the following two points: one's own pure conscience;[23] and the great justice[24] by which the sovereigns and subjects are ethically bound to each other.[25] This one single pure conscience is the common fundamental property of the ruling monarch above and of the common people under him, existing from the earliest age of the gods till the present day and from the present day to the most distant future, co-eternal with the heavens and the earth."[26]

St. Jiun, in his interpretation of the classics, gives rational and symbolical explanations and tries to make the people of the Tokugawa period understand advanced philosophical and ethical ideas in them.[27]

Natural law should be the basis for ethical conduct throughout all countries. "Just as heaven and earth exist, so also are there various countries in existence. Sun, moon, and stars move according to the laws of heaven, while mountains, seas and rivers are governed by the laws of earth. As there are various countries, so there exist men to inhabit them. The human nexus is constituted by the relationships between lord and subject, parents and children, husband and wife, between brothers, and between friends."[28]

However, Jiun was not a law scholar. Whereas GROTIUS made a quite extraordinary impression on the statesmen of the seventeenth and eighteenth centuries, and influenced later legal thought, Jiun was an individual thinker and his thought was forgotten.

ISHIDA Baigan, the founder of the Shingaku school, admitted Nature, which is good. "A healthy person can taste food and enjoy it, but a man sick with fever even if he does eat, cannot taste good food and so does not enjoy it. The people who do not understand Good Nature are like that."[29] Using the technical terms of the Neo-Confucianists of the Sung period, he explains Nature: "The movement of the Forms is the ever spreading Ether of Heaven and Earth. As it can be clearly seen that Heaven and Earth and myself are single, harmonious thing, we can deduce that the theory of Good Nature is evident and in agreement with the Doctrine of Changes."[30]

Our human individual is a microcosm, and in this sense it partakes of Nature. "Inspiration and Expiration are negative and positive. Those who follow this are good. The Internal Substance which rules the deeds of our External Functioning is Nature. From this you can see that, man, as a whole, is a small Heaven and Earth. If you fully conceive your being as a small Heaven and Earth, you will never complain for lack of anything."[31]

In the behavioral context it can be called Human-Heartedness. "The peace of one's mind is Human-Heartedness. Human-Heartedness is Heaven's original Ether. This Ether from Heaven generates and keeps alive all these Thousand Things. The aim and the reason for learning is to get to know one's mind. Our duty is to feed nature through our mind while we breathe. If we follow the Way of Human-Heartedness and Love and Propriety even a little, we may live in peace."[32]

Considered in terms of the Forms, another term of the Neo-Confucianists, Nature is called the Mind. "It is the Mind which identifies itself in the Forms. See how the Mind exists even in birds and animals! Frogs are naturally afraid of snakes. It is not surely a mother who teaches her offspring that snakes are dangerous and will gobble them up and, of course, tadpoles do not study and do not gradually learn all this. The fact is that if you are born under the Form of a frog, the fear for snakes comes straight in the Mind from the Form. Let us consider something analogous: when summer comes a flea clings to man's body. Here again, do a flea's parents teach it to live by sucking men's blood? Is it taught if it sees a man's hand approach, it must jump away immediately lest it lose its life? The reason is that when a flea jumps away it acts in accordance with the Forms and not because it has learnt to do so."[33] "Birds and beasts have no Personal Mind and therefore comply perfectly with the dictates of the Forms."[34] The explanation of nature with these illustrations is not so different from that of the West. But it seems that Nature was equated with the Mind by him. "What is called Nature is the Internal Substance of Heaven, of Earth and Man."[35]

The final goal of ethical conduct was, according to him, to recover one's own original Mind. "To attain something by following the Law means to attain the Mind."[36] "If you just let yourself go, and become receptive, everything is natural, easy, evident."[37] One might be surprised, when he knows that he wants to apply his theory even to politics. "By ruling without acknowledging this Order (Principle) a ruler will not be able to govern his country."[38] His thought may sound too idealistic, but when we find a highly idealistic Western counterpart in FICHTE, we need not be surprised.

The same inclination can be noticed in aesthetics also. Discussing Sanskrit and Dutch poetry *together,* MIURA Baien was led to a conviction that there exists some universal aesthetical principles valid for poetry

Eastern and Western. He concludes: "From this it may be seen that all that is in accordance with the essence of things never deviates from the one path."[39]

NINOMIYA Sontoku, the "Peasant Sage," emphasized the indebtedness of mankind to nature and to fellowship. Man's true nature, Sontoku taught, consists in pious devotion to the order of nature, which manifests itself in the moral order of human life, especially in the relation between the lord and his subjects, parents and children, benefactor and recipient in general, expressed in grace and gratitude. Nature evolves and changes by itself, but man has to conquer his instinctive selfishness and endeavor to conform to the moral order of life.[40] Contrary to the general trend of naturalism, NINOMIYA Sontoku emphasized frugality, which is an outcome of the sense of indebtedness, and gratitude for the benefit bestowed.

The most radical conception of Nature was held by ANDŌ Shōeki, who said: "It is erroneous to designate as 'the Way' various teachings such as Confucianism, Buddhism, Shintoism, Taoism, and medicine. By the Way ought to be implied the single motivating power of Nature, that is the unique principle of practical virtue."[41] He severely criticized traditional religions. "Saints (or sages) of all ages stole Heaven's way, made arbitrary institutions out of it, sold benevolence and righteousness, bought (i.e., received) taxes, and ate and dressed by so doing. The saints' followers sold the laws of the saints and bought the world of avarice to eat and dress without labor."[42]

The terms 'law' and 'natural law' had been used from antiquity on, and we find it rather difficult to discern the difference between the ancient and the modern usage of these terms. This point should be subjected to further study.

The Idea of Evolution

The idea of nature or natural law was common to both East and West. But what was lacking in Eastern countries was the idea of evolution. There were the ideas of change, manifestation and development there. But people there did not think of evolution clearly. The idea of evolution appeared first in the modern West. It seems that this idea did not

occur in Eastern countries prior to the introduction of Western civilization, although its influence has been very strong since then.

In correspondence with this feature, dialectical thinking was not clear
in Eastern countries before the introduction of Western civilization. The
T'ien-t'ai and San-lun philosophies of ancient China and Japan had some
dialectical thinking, but it did not develop in the line of dialectics. In
modern Japan there were some individual thinkers who held some dialectical ideas. ISHIDA Baigan set forth the thought that Negative and
Positive are two things and yet they cannot be separated. But even if it
seems one, it has the two aspects of Motion and Quiescence.[43]

MIURA Baien (1723–1789) expressed a theory of dialectic of his own.
The way to understand nature (or the universe) is dialectics (*jōri*). The
secret (*ketsu*) of dialectics is to see synthesis (*gōitsu*) in antithesis (*han*). It
is to give up one-sided preoccupation and to correct marks (*chōhyō*). *Yin*
and *Yang* are antithetical to each other, and constitute a battle. As they
are antithetic to each other they can be brought to synthesis.[44] He said:
"The way to see things thoroughly (*takkan*) is logic (*jōri*) and the essence
of logic is nothing else but the dialectic of antithesis and synthesis
(*hankan gōitsu*), setting aside all attachments of mind and following the
correct signs."[45] The three elements, then, that go into the full structure
of MIURA's *jōri* are the dialectic of things, the prerequisite eliminations
of bias and preoccupation, and finally, the empirical test.[46]

Here we find the thought of dialectics in its incipient stage. But his
opinion was not set forth so systematically as the system of HEGEL.

3. Changes in the Valuation of Traditional Symbols

The Problems

Modern valuation of man begins with the discarding of charismatic
authorities in general. Moderns generally do not admit the significance
of particular men who are qualified with higher magical or spiritual
power by birth or by esoteric practice.

To this fundamental attitude there are three corollaries:

(1) Denunciation of esoteric religious practices which are regarded as

endowing the practitioner with charismatic authority. Here "esoteric" means "to be intended for only a secluded group of disciples or inmates who are qualified by a religious authority."

(2) Denunciation of the charisma of a particular person who has been given prestige by peculiar practices authorized by something above men. "Charisma" means possessing certain extraordinary, divine power which inspire people to follow a specific pattern of behavior laid down by an authority.

(3) Denunciation of systems of esoteric religious practices, which have tended to be formalistic. Denunciation of esoteric religious austerities was the starting-point for the development of modern thought.

Denunciation of Religious Formalism and Stress on Inner Devotion

The esteem of religious rites is based upon the attention paid to the outer symbolical expression of our religious feeling. Stereotyped symbols do not necessarily express human values. The effort then to recover oneself as man implies the devaluation of esoteric or formalistic religious rites and symbol, and stress on inner devotion.

However, it was only independent individuals who expressed the attitude of iconoclasm. For example, Mokujiki (1718–1810), the itinerant, said:

> "My voice has become hoarse
> Due to repetition of Nembutsu prayers
> But, alas, no reply!
> Amida and Shakya Buddha are taking a siesta!"[47]

Therefore, iconoclasm did not occur as a nation-wide movement among Japanese Buddhists. A work entitled *Daijingū Sankeiki* (The Diary of a Pilgrim to Ise Shrine) by SAKA Shibutsu, father of Jubutsu, runs as follows:

> "It is quite usual with us and it is of great significance, that we do not carry with us any rosaries like Buddhists and we do not present any material offerings to the Sun Goddess at Ise; in other words, there is no selfish desire or petition on our part. This is called inner purity or heart-purity. We worshippers cleanse ourselves with lustral water

ceremonially; we call this outer purity or bodily purity. So purified, without and within, we are all-purity itself like the Divinity. The deity is immanent in man and man is inherent in the deity; there is neither the divine nor the human; there is no difference in essence at all between them. When I the author was so told by the Shinto priest at the Shrine of the Sun Goddess, I was overwhelmed with tears of pious gratitude."[48]

WATARAI Nobuyoshi (died in 1690) said: "Complete sincerity is the absolute principle of Shintoism."[49] The new Shinto sects which appeared at the end of the Tokugawa period showed a strong tendency to discard all doctrinal subtleties and complicated ritualism, and to establish a religion of the simple pure heart. On the occasion of the Meiji Restoration fanatic nationalists took images of Buddhas and Bodhisattvas and copies of scriptures out of Buddhist temples, and burnt them. But this was not a movement which occurred from within Japanese Buddhism itself, but which was instigated by aggressive Shinto revivalists. Shinto iconoclasm was carried out within its own tradition without any religious influence from abroad.

Religious rites can be regarded as symbols, in essential respects, expressing and communicating one's own religious feelings and will to act in accordance with religious values. But they themselves should not be regarded as absolute, however long they may have been traditionally observed. If they come to bind and hamper men, they cease to be such. Some modern thinkers of Japan took this view, and tried to restore the basis upon which religious symbols exist.

Denunciation of the Charismatic Authority of an Individual

In the Medieval Ages, both in the East and West, spiritual teachers claimed special authority over their diciples and followers. They assumed the role of superior men and were regarded as higher than common people. Very often they served as living gods or deputies of God or gods.

Such an attitude was criticized very often by Zen masters, but not necessarily in modern times. One of the religious leaders of modern

Japan who is noteworthy in this connexion is SUZUKI Shōsan who denied the authority of the founders and previous masters of various sects. He said: "Looking into written sayings of previous masters, it does not seem that there have been persons who have practiced with zeal."[50]

Master Munan, explaining the phrase: "Transmission outside the doctrines," said

"As the essence of religion lies originally outside of the doctrines, we cannot help. It was a big blunder that Lord Shakya taught the excellent teaching!"[51]

Here a Zen master actually admonishes the founder of Buddha!

ANDŌ Shōeki judged Confucian scholars and Buddhist clergy as the spiritual oppressors of his age, in the same way as WINSTANLEY decried the clergy and lawyers as the chief deceivers of the people. Yet neither Shōeki nor WINSTANLEY can be properly termed atheists. The one preserved a veneration for the genial gods of old Japan and, like a pantheist, he seems to have equated them with the forces of Nature; the other, puritan and protestant, looked to the Scriptures as his sole guide to morality and political practice.[52]

In order to ridicule the secluded life of recluses, Munan tested recluses, saying: "One who will become a recluse in mountains without attaining enlightenment is due to become a beast!"[53]

Denunciation of Religious Differences

The attitude of denouncing charismatic and scriptural authority, on the one hand, and that of denouncing religious rites, on the other hand, led thinkers to reject differences between religions.

This tendency occurred among reformative religious leaders of Japan at nearly the same period as in the West. Tenkei, the liberal Sōtō Zen teacher, did not deny the distinction between various sects,[54] but he denied distinctions such as Rinzai, Sōtō, etc. in Zen Buddhism. Tenkei, being a monk of Sōtō Zen, eliminated or criticized the passages in Dōgen's works in which Master Dōgen, the founder of Japanese Sōtō Zen, praised the lineage of Sōtō, and rejected the lineage of Rinzai. It would be difficult to think of his liberal attitude apart from his social background that he preached in the city of Osaka, the most prosperous commercial center of Japan. Most Shingaku teachers taught Buddhism in general. Kyūō (1783–1839) said:

"Different sects look up to the same moon shining on the summit. . . . Each one should keep the teaching of one's own sect carefully, and endeavor not to compute with others."[55]

When the above-mentioned standpoint is theoretically pushed to the extreme, the distinction between various religions should be abolished. Master Munan said: "Mind is called Gods, Heaven or Buddha in three countries (i.e., Japan, China and India). Their terms are different, but the same in essence."[56]

We find the same echo in the campaign of Confucianists also. Itō Jinsai (1627–1705) said: "From the viewpoint of scholars there is in fact Confucianism and Buddhism; from the viewpoint of the Universe there is properly neither Confucianism nor Buddhism; there is but One Way and that is all!"[57]

When we come to think further theoretically, what is called a religion itself comes to be useless. Mokujiki, the itinerant priest, blamed the narrow attitude of sectarianism.

"It would be useless to be staunchly devout to Buddhism; When I asked Dear Amida (about what Buddhism is), he replied: O! Conglomeration of falsehood!"[58]

Ishida Baigan asserted that one should foresake the specific appellation of each religion. "When you have attained the Mind, you are free from either the names of Buddhism or of Confucianism."[59] "There are no different Minds and whoever believes that thanks to Buddhism he can attain a different Mind, is foolish, and will never come to any good."[60] Both the Shingaku movement originating from Ishida Baigan and the Hōtoku movement originating from Ninomiya Sontoku, were more or less eclectic and attempted to extract from various religions what was most essential to religion and beneficial to practical ethics and popular instruction. This feature can be found in the thought of Master Jiun, the pioneer of Sanskrit scholarship also.

In spite of these new movements, however, denominational boundaries were strictly laid down by the Tokugawa Government, and over-stepping them was prohibited.

In the field of religion highly liberal movements such as unitarianism or universalism occurred. The Shingaku scholars of Japan advocated that Mind alone is the basis of religion and minimized all authorities.

Every dogmatic religion overlooks the practical significance of symbols, and worships not only images but also theological opinions. These are nothing but the outer symbols of the absolute. These forms are employed by religions only to focus their faith. When the worshippers confuse these outer symbols with the deeper true reality, they get into idolatry.

The current diverse religious groups which are bound within themselves by means of dogmas, rites, and ceremonies, militate against the formation of a universal human society. If we realize the true significance of symbolism, then we shall not insist on any one route by which men reach knowledge of reality or truth. To reject the differences between religions, follows logically from a higher valuation of man.

It seems that such a non-sectarian tendency was easier to appear in Eastern countries than in the West. However, all movements of such a tendency had a stumbling block. Any new religious movement of this kind was based upon, so to speak, the greatest common measure of the several existing religions which were prevalent in those days. So any non-sectarian movement had to face the ironical danger that the movement itself tended to be sectarian at the end.

4. Changes in the Valuation of Man

Value of Man as the Supreme—Stress on Human Love

The ethics of esteeming man as such presupposes man as the supreme value. Some expect that faith in God leads to the realization of it, while others do not assume God and yet try to attain to the same realization. In either case love or compassion directed to others was regarded as the first principle of human action.

This attitude was emphasized also by some contemporaneous thinkers in Japan, who did not have belief in the Son of God.

In Christianity the relationship between Christ and his followers is sometimes explained in comparison to that which exists between bride and bridegroom. From this point of view, Kabir's mental attitude towards faith shares some common features with Western religion rather than with ancient Brahmanism and Buddhism.

Among Chinese and Japanese Buddhists, however, even in the modern ages, the idea of lover-sweetheart relationship never came into being, while the idea of compassion has been greatly extolled. Such a concept would have been deemed rather secular in China and Japan.

According to modern thinkers, love replaces everything. Their insistence on the spirit of emphasizing love or compassion is such that it becomes the basis of all kinds of moral action and eventually raises the valuation of man.

Some modern thinkers asserted that man's sinfulness is justified for the sake of the glory of God.

Such an assertion was not entertained by contemporaneous thinkers in China, Japan or other Asian countries, for Buddhism does not presuppose creation by God, and consequently there was no need to justify it.

In China and Japan of the same period, a tendency to set forth the esteem of love in the form of esteeming the physical nature of human being was in existence.

In modern Japan Confucianists tried to accept man's natural dispositions against the traditions of Chinese Confucianism and Buddhism. Ogyū Sorai recognized the intrinsic value latent in Japanese novels, in spite of their immoral contents.[61] Dazai Shuntai called man's natural feelings the real feelings, which he defined to be "likes and dislikes, sufferings and rejoicing, and anxiety and pleasure, etc." And he went on to maintain". . . . There is not a single human being devoid of these feelings. . . . Love of one's parents, wife and children is also the same among the noble and the common. Since these feelings are originated in the innate truthfulness of man which is free from any stain of sin or falsity, they are called the real feelings."[62] His standpoint was pure naturalism. "There are no double-dealings in the deeds motivated by the overflow of the natural dispositions, wherein no discrepancy between intentions and deeds is caused; the inside and outside are so transparent that reality and appearance are one and the same thing. The natural dispositions are the innate and true nature of man."[63] He defiantly declared: "I would rather be a master of acrobatic feats, than to be a moralist."[64] Although there was no systematic philosophical basis for the existing affirmative attitude, the spirit of the Japanese people prior to the entry of Buddhism can be characterized as a mode of natural affirmation. And this feature was emphasized by scholars of Japanese classics.[65]

MOTOORI Norinaga (1730–1801), refuting Confucianism and Buddhism, said:

"The pure mind is the natural mind." "The Confucian scholars who are most highly esteemed as men of wisdom, and the Buddhist priests who are revered as saints, admire the beauty of stars and flowers, but they pretend never to have taken notice of a beautiful woman. What a deception of mind!"[66]

"They hate the natural inclinations of man, but are not these same inclinations the devine laws?"[67]

In such words of MOTOORI there sounds unmistakably the same feeling of joy and love of nature and man as was proclaimed in the European Renaissance. HIRATA Atsutane (1766–1843), the founder of Jingoistic Shintoism, said: "To comply with the natural dispositions is called the Way . . . Man is born provided with the innate true feelings of benevolence, justice, propriety and intelligence. Not to falsify or not to distort them is the true way of humanity. . . . One should indeed stop acting like a sage and abandon the so-called Mind or the way of enlightenment, and all that are affected and Buddhaish.

Onkō (Jiun Sonja), a modern Buddhist thinker, preached that morality means to follow man's natural dispositions.[68] TOKUGAWA Nariaki, the nationalist leader who attempted the revival of Confucian scholarship in the late feudal age of Japan, said: "What is spreading the Way (Kōdō)? It is man himself that can spread the Way."[69] It is noteworthy that ISHIDA Baigan came to point out that saints and ordinary men are not essentially different with respect to human nature. "All men are gifted with the immutable mind, but blinded by the Seven Emotions they believe that a Saint has some peculiar wisdom of his own which differes from any other wisdom of ordinary mortals, and due to their blindness they are filled with doubts."[70] Miki (1798–1887) of Yamato, the founder of the Tenrikyō religion taught that the human being is the abode of devine charity.

Corresponding to this new trend Buddhist masters came to reject the former attitude of asceticism. Master Hakuin (1685–1768) said: " 'To cast away oneself' does not mean 'ill-treat oneself' or 'to disregard diet and health.' "[71] Moreover, a new trend occurred in Buddhism also. Master Jiun said: "What is called man is gifted with the Ten Virtues and at the same time the world of humanity is by nature endowed with Ten Virtues. . . . One should have cognizance of man in contrast to animals."[72] And then he elaborates on the distinction between the two. In the mediaeval ages Japanese Buddhists were apt to lay more emphasis on the virtue of compassion, which should extend to animals, than on the superiority of man over animals. But here a reformist Buddhist leader accentuates the dignity and significance of man.

As a corollary from the thought that man is the supreme, cruel punishments and customs, such as burning at the stake and duelling, which were prevalent in both East and West, became extinct although the date of extinction differed from country to country. With the dying of religious fantasticism, Buddhist monks no longer burned themselves on alters as sacrifices to Buddha, as in the mediaeval ages, in China and Japan. The attitude of some Zen masters became more lenient towards the sins of their disciples.[73]

Humanistic attitude as was mentionend above was given further accentuation and became an advantageous weapon to refute Christianity. Contrasting the Christian idea of the supreme God with Confucianism which was his own standpoint in this context, Baien says: "The Way of the Sages does indeed revere and venerate Heaven, but it is a doctorine of human ethics."[74] The anti-transcendent and society-centered ethics was forcifully stressed by him.[75]

But the humanitarian attitude in the modern ages was different from the attitude of mediaeval compassion. In Japan the practical observance of this mediaeval ideal had to be circumscribed within narrow bounds. For example, ISHIDA Baigan said: "If you try to realize the Way of government only through the fulfillment of the spirit of compassion and love and disregard the Saint's Law, rebellions will be the only result."[76] Thus the general tendency of humanitarian spirit developed in a rather realistic way.[77]

Equality of Man—Anti-discrimination

The rigidity of the class system (shi-nō-kō-shō or samurai-farmer manufacturer-trader) already began to show signs of collapse by the end of the 18th century, even before the official nullification of it at the time of the Meiji Restoration.[78]

The attitude of esteeming man as such leads one to discard all discriminations established upon the traditional authority. Already in mediaeval Japan religious leaders advocated the equality of man in the religious sense. Shinran did not admit that women are less capable than men of attaining to the state of bliss. Nichiren (1222–1282) found one of the justifications for his belief in the Lotus Sūtra in its teaching of equality of the sexes. The Oral (Esoteric) teachings of the Japanese Tendai Sect advocated the equality of all mankind.[79] But their recognition of man's equality remained in the narrow bounds of the religious interpretation and did not develop into a social movement.

While the Western modern period was in progress, the cry for equality in Japan was not so loud as in the West or even in India. Even brilliant Buddhist leaders such as Master Jiun who was so progressive in other respects acquiesced in the existing hierarchical social system of Japan in those days. Master Jiun's own interpretation of the Buddhist teaching of equality is as follows: "Buddhism approves distinctions of grade and position. The equality it teaches is not such foolishness as that of breaking down high mountains, filling in deep valleys and making all into a dead level. Buddhism teaches us the way between lord and subjects, father and son, master and disciple."[80] But it does not follow that this standpoint of this shows his backwardness, for in the modern West also the regulations concerning these distinctions were enforced, which look quite backward in the eye of people of the present day.

In Japan before the introduction of the Western civilization there were Buddhist thinkers who advocated theories which implied equality of men. The author of the *Saru-hōgo* (Sermon by a monkey) denounced the concept of private property in the religious sense. "You should not make discrimination between self and others. Riches such as gold, silver, fortune and treasures are the common property of the whole world. Even if they are in the hands of others, they do not belong to them. Even if I keep them, they are not mine. If they are confined in the hands of others without being utilized, they are of no use; if I do not utilize them, solely keeping grip of them, it is like piling up stones."[81] Munan, a Zen priest, discouraged the custom of leaving property to one's own descendants. "You should not bequeath treasures to your children. It is certain that they are wasted. To practise the teaching of Buddha is most important."[82] They asserted that riches should be used for the benefit of the public. But their existence in society was marginal and hardly attracted any serious attention. In Eastern countries few attempts were made to bring the ideal of equality into practice. It was only with the advent of Western forces that the feudal system of Japan collapsed.

In Japan under the Tokugawa government women were not given equal status with men. But towards the end of the Tokugawa feudal regime, there appeared prophetesses who founded new religions such as Isson-kyō, Tenri-kyō. This reminds us of the fact that a conspicuous religious phenomenon after World War II is the rise of new religions. Among a total of 120, about 48 were founded by ladies. This phenomenon cannot be found in pre-modern Japan.

This-Worldliness

The principle of esteeming man as such and loving men as equal beings tends to obliterate the attitude that takes it for granted to subject men to and sacrifice for any higher being, including God or gods.

The general tendency of religious thought in the mediaeval age throughout many countries can be described as being other-worldly.

Happiness people yearned for in those days was the one which was believed to exist only in the future world after death, the supposed Heaven.

In Japan the turning-point from other-worldliness to this-worldliness seems to have occurred around the Kambun period (1661–1673). Prior to that period, i.e., in the early Tokugawa period, printed books were published at the rate of Buddhist 3 : non-Buddhist 1. But after this period the rate was reversed due to the fact that the circulation of printed books on Confucianism gradually increased. Buddhism suffered criticism for its other-worldliness by Japanese Confucianists and scholars of Japanese classics. Some reformist Buddhists changed their traditional attitude. The this-worldly character of Zen in the modern times was conspicuous in such Zen priests as Suzuki Shōsan who taught lay believers: "To pray for a happy future does not mean to pray for a world after death. It means to be delivered here and now and thus to attain a great comfort. Then, where do you think the afflictions of this world come from? They are originated from your attachment to your own flesh and to the demands of it. To be delivered from this attachment is the way to become a Buddha."[83] But such a doctrine was not generally accepted in the Tokugawa period.

Humanitarianism bears close reference to the attitude of this-worldliness, and is one of the conspicuous features that exerted no small influence upon the evaluation of man in the modern times.

In Japanese Buddhism there appeared some reformists who affirmed human life on this side of heaven. Master Jiun said: "Some say that, since Buddhism urges only the disciplines of the mind by the mind's own capacity, it is of no use to the common people and of no value to those who govern them. Confucianism, which is said to teach the regulation of conduct by forms, ceremonies and rules of etiquette, is of great service in teaching and edifying people. This objection is made by those who do not really know what Buddhism is, and have seen only its shortcomings which arose after the dynasties of Sung and Yuan. Buddhism is the true Law, and the practical observance of its teachings, the Ten Virtues, enables even ordinary men to regulate themselves and their home, and finally walk in the path of righteousness."

However, the life-affirming attitude was more obviously found among non-Buddhists. According to KUROZUMI Munetada (1780–1850), the founder of the Kurozumi Sect of Shintoism, the significance of human life consists in a realization of our intrinsic connection with the cosmic vitality. This communion he denominated *iki-tōshi*, i.e., "penetrating into life" or "pervaded by vitality." ANDŌ Shōeki declared: "Direct cultivation and happy eating, direct weaving and happy clothing—there is no Way but this. Talking of thousands of ways is false."[84] But the avowal of such an outspoken assertion was not permitted under the pressure of the Tokugawa Shogunate government. It was only after the Meiji Restoration that freedom to express one's opinion publicly became possible, but sometimes with the probability of harsh censure on the side of educators and social leaders.

The Esteem of Activity in Society and Vocational Ethics

As earthly life consists in action, the attitude of this-worldliness tends to emphasize action in social life. (*vita activa versus vita contemplativa*.)

In Japan the spirit of activity was extolled.

As Dōgen criticized and metamorphosed Chinese Zen in the medieval age, so ITŌ Jinsai (1627–1705), a Japanese Confucianist, amended the form of Chinese neo-Confucianism to answer his purpose. To Jinsai the intrinsic nature of both earth and heaven lies in their activeness which we would term evolutionary. Eternal development is the only and true existence. Jinsai completely denies what is called death.

The *Book of Changes* (I Ching) says, "The great virtue of heaven and earth is called life." It means that living without ceasing is th very way of heaven and earth. Because the way of heaven and earth is one with life, there exist life without death and convergence without divergence. Though the bodies of ancestors may perish, their spirits are inherited by their children, whose spirits are also handed down to their own children. When life thus evolves from generation to generation, without ceasing, through all eternity, it may be rightly said that no one dies.[85]

ITŌ Jinsai believes that the world of reality consists of change and action and that action is in itself good. "Between heaven and earth there is only one reason: motion without stillness, good without evil. Stillness is the end of motion, while evil is the change of good; and good is a kind of life, while evil is a kind of death. It is not that these two opposites are generated together, but they are all one with life."[86]

Itō Jinsai's younger contemporary Ogyū Sorai, though a rival to Jinsai, does not grudge his admiration for Jinsai's activities, calling them "the supreme knowledge of a thousand years," and denounces the static character of the Chinese school of Li. In fact it can be said that all of the characteristic Japanese scholars believe in phenomena as the fundamental mode of existence. They unanimously rejected the quietism of the Confucianists of Medieaval China (the Sung period).[87] Quiet sitting and fostering reverential love in one's heart used to be the method of mental training practised by most Chinese Confucianists of the Middle Ages (around the Sung period). Sorai ridiculed those Confucianists and said: "As I look at them, even gambling seems to be superior to quiet sitting and fostering reverential love in one's heart."[88]

Meditation was repudiated even by some Zen masters notwithstanding that the quintessence of their religion would be in the practice of meditation. Suzuki Shōsan discouraged laymen from practising meditation; instead he encouraged them in their faithful performance of daily duties.

The encouragement of the spirit of activity was conspicuous especially among the merchants whose influence was gradually permeating the society. Ishida Baigan, one of their ideological leaders and the founder of the Shingaku movement, said: "Once Confucius stood by a river and said;[89] 'It flows on just like this, never ceasing day and night!' He means that a flowing river is the best possible means to penetrate the Internal Substance of the Way."[90] This somewhat twisted interpretation was similar to that which was given by Itō Jinsai.[91] Confucius lamented the transitoriness of all things under the sun by the saying, but Jinsai took it for his extolment of the activeness of generations and development of all things.

This characteristic willingness to accept the phenomenal world as given and to live contentedly in it was not confined exclusively to Buddhism and Confucianism in Japan. It is found in modern pre-Meiji Shintoism as well. The founder of the Konkō Sect teaches: "Whether alive or dead, you should regard the heaven and earth as your own habitation."[92]

This spirit finally became the motivating power for the modernization of Japan. The new religions whose appearance dates around the turning-point leading to the collapse of the feudal regime entertained the same notion. Here is a little anecdote of KUROZUMI Munetada who had been severely ill with consumption for a long time. It was in 1874 when he was at the age of thirty four. On the morning of the winter solstice, while worshipping the rising sun, he was suddenly awakened mentally and bodily to complete recovery from his chronic disease. TOKUGAWA Nariaki, one of the instigators for the Meiji Restoration, insisted upon the importance of the spirit of activity. "How can we Japanese subjects of the Emperor remain inactive without undertaking the propaganda of this Way and without revealing to the world the virtuous merits of our ancestors? It is with this aim in view that this Institute has been founded." It may be said that there is little disparity in substance between this attitude and the national consciousness in other countries in the modern ages, save that the aim of Nariaki's action lay in "revering the Emperor and expelling the barbarians." In this case he meant by "barbarians" Westerners.

On the other hand, there was a thinker isolated from the current of the time. ANDŌ Shōeki advocated The Way of Nature and Labour.[93] He protested against exploitation by feudal lords. He appreciated the exultation of agriculture and sympathized with peasants for their miserable condition under the oppression of feudal lords.

According to NORMAN, Shōeki has two counterparts in the West. One is François QUESNAY (1694–1774), a French encyclopédiste, and the most famous of the Physiocrats. Both lived at nearly the same time; both were physicians but agriculture was their real delight.[94] Just as QUESNAY found in China the exemplification of the natural order, so Shōeki in the reverse direction turned to Europe for one of the model states he pictured to himself.[95] The other counterpart, Gerrard WINSTANLEY was also a spokesman for the underprivileged and impoverished section of the community, the evicted tenant, the precarious day labourer, the copy holder vainly struggling against the onslaught of the landlord who proceeded with enclosure.[96] Thus he paid due attention to labouring people and in this respect he has something in common with Saint-Simon (1768–1825), who asserted that the ultimate aim was the rise, both in intellect and economy, of the working class, the class which suffered most.

A corollary from the attitude of esteeming activity was to denounce the life of monks. Mediaeval layistic leaders such as Shinran still held respect and esteem for the monks who were leading an ascetic life. They held those monks to be superior to themselves. But in the modern age some activistic thinkers despised monks for their indolence and inactivity. NINOMIYA disliked priests and scholars in general because in his opinion, they were not producers, and so did not add to the prosperity of the country.[97]

In this connexion, the Buddhist custom of mendicancy or living by begging alms became the target of severe criticism of Japanese Confucianists, and gradually died out.

It is noteworthy that the above-mentioned trend of emphasizing activity is so similar to that of the West.[98]

In Shintoism there was an idea called "Yosashi" which is an equivalent of "mikoto-mochite,"[99] its literal meaning being "by (the grace of) calling by God." It etymologically coincide with the Western concept of 'vocation,' or 'Beruf.' Shintoists based their own vocational ethics on this concept,[100] 'calling.'

Towards the modern period of Japan there occurred a theory that if a man pursues his own secular vocation with his whole heart and soul, he is practising nothing other than the ascetic practice of Buddhism.

Takuan (1573–1645), a Zen priest, taught: "The Law of the Buddha, well observed, is identical with the Law of mundane existence. The Law of mundane existence, well observed, is identical with the Law of Buddha."[101] This idea was especially stressed by SUZUKI Shōsan, another Zen priest, who claimed to be the first man to apply Buddhism to matters of mundane existence. He wrote a book entitled *Bammin Tokuyō* (The Significance of Everyman's Activities), in which he discussed problems of vocational ethics. He found absolute significance in the pursuit of any vocation, whether it be that of a warrior, a farmer, a craftman, a merchant, a doctor, an actor, a hunter, or a priest. He reasoned that to pursue one's own vocation is to obey the Absolute One because the essence of Buddhism consists in reliance upon the guidance of the original self or upon "the true Buddha of one's own" and every vocation is the function of this "one Buddha." Thus he preached to farmers: "Farming is nothing but the doings of a Buddha."[102] To merchants he taught: "Renounce desires and pursue profits single-heartedly. But you should never enjoy the fruit of your labors. You should, instead, work for the good of all others." Since afflictions of this world, it is said, are predestined in former worlds, one should torture oneself by working hard at one's own vocation, in order to redeem the sins committed in one's former life.[103] It is noteworthy that, immediately after the death of CALVIN, an idea similar to his appeared almost contemporaneously in Japan. The fact, however, that it never grew into a religious movement of great consequence ought to be studied in relation to the underdevelopment of a modern *bourgeois* society in Japan.

To YOKOI Shōnan (1809–69), one of the most progressive thinkers of Japan during the latter half of the Tokugawa regime (1840–67), Christianity was a religion which was perfectly congruous with the materialistic mind of the West. Shōnan attributed the western virtue of hard work to Christianity and in this respect he perceived in Christianity something analoguous to what is known as the protestant ethics.[104]

A Japanese counterpart of the predestination theory by Dutch Calvinists is found in the teachings of the Nyorai-kyō religion founded by a prophetess called Kino (died 2 May 1826).[105]

A change to asceticism practiced by means of faithful performance of duties in mundane existence appeared in a much wider circle of Shinshū believers. In the early period Shinshū stressed salvation by faith alone and paid little attention to ethical demands, but by the middle of the Tokugawa period ethical action came to be regarded as a pre-condition for salvation and no more was heard about the wicked being saved. Thus ethical action became the very sign of salvation.[106]

The Hōtoku (lit. 'To Return Virtues') teaching, which was derived from the teaching of NINOMIYA Sontoku and was addressed especially to agricultural population, emphasized energy and work. The purport of his teaching is as follows: "We owe our life and its preservation and enjoyment first to the benefits granted by Heaven and Creation, then to those we receive from our sovereign, our country, our parents, and other sources innumerable. We have laws and social obligations which compel us to return, in some degree, the benefits received from parents, sovereign, and country; but there are no laws obliging us to render our gratitude by actions for the greater benefits bestowed on us by Heaven; therefore men are prone to forget that requital for the heavenly benefits is their first duty, and neglect it. Some indeed remember, but generally they think it enough to show their gratitude by ceremonies of worship and thanksgiving, and not by deeds. This should not be so. We must bear the will of Heaven in mind, and try to cultivate Heaven-sent virtue in us and work earnestly to promote the progress and the development of all creation. We find that even the great success of industrial capitalism in modern Japan is readily traced to the diligence of the common people, whose moral background is rooted in the teachings of NINOMIYA Sontoku, an original philosopher-economist of the late Tokugawa period.

The moral-economic philosophy of NINOMIYA with its four fundamentals, faith, labour, economy and charity, may have been favourable to fair capitalist competition, although his influence remained chiefly among peasants. In pre-War days, patronized by the nation and adapted to its educational policy, his spirit dominated the national education in moral practice throughout the country. But the rise of capitalism in Japan after the Meiji Restoration should be viewed in a wider context.

Lay Tendencies in Religion

This-worldliness tends to liberate religion from the exclusive possession of the priesthood. We have to first take Shinran into consideration for research on the tendency to implant religion in the mind and life of the laity. Although Shinran belongs to the mediaeval age, his life and activities have so many points in common with LUTHER, especially in the respect of lay religion.[107]

Shinran learned the traditional Tendai theology at the Hieizan monastery which was the scholarly centre of Japanese Buddhism. But he found himself at an impasse when his earnest practice of meditation led him nowhere and all carnal desires and mental afflictions remained with him. Shinran felt that his efforts had been in vain. He had practiced asceticism, unsparing of pains and absorbed in speculation, only to come to the conclusion that, notwithstanding all that had been done and all his faith in himself, he had advanced not a single step nearer the goal. He said to himself: "It grows dark, but the goal is still far off! Now there is but one way left to save my soul. I must seek for divine guidance."[108] He turned to Kwannon, the Buddhist counterpart of Mary, for his spiritual rest. He confined himself to the Rokkaku-dō temple and prayed to the Kwannon enshrined in it for days and nights, until Kwannon revealed herself to him and had him study under Hōnen (1133–1212), the founder of Pure Land Buddhism who taught him that one can be saved solely by the grace and compassion of Amida Buddha.

Concerning Shinran's marriage[109] there are some legends, but at any rate he spent a married life like the early Protestant leaders, and was the father of several children. Since then his followers have all married. Shinran combined religion with a layman's life.

It was noteworthy that in Japanese Buddhism as in Christianity there was a Protestant Reformation. Both Hōnen and Shinran, who is the more radical reformer of the two, cut themselves off from the abuses of the established sects just as LUTHER and CALVIN did in Europe. In both cases the central principle was salvation by faith, not by works or ceremonies.

Pure Land Buddhism professed by them embodies the extreme doctrine of salvation by faith in Amida, the Buddha of Boundless Light. This doctrine parallels the doctrine of absolute reliance on God as stated in the Augsburg Confession. They said that faith in Amida arouses a new motive and refreshes a feeling of gratitude which transforms life. Both in Japan and in Europe these religious reformations were accompanied by social, political and economic phenomena. There was the same sort of lay movement started, the same sort of protest against the ascetic life of the monastic type, and the same encouragement of marriage, labour, and social activity, although it was only after the advent of Rennyo (1415-1499) that social activity became conspicuous. The political implications, however, were much more marked in the West than in Japan in proportion as the emphasis on faith as opposed to works was more extreme in Pure Land Buddhism than in Christianity.

Shinran and Vallabha,[110] an Indian religious reformer, came to be worshipped as divine in later days, and the successors of both, who were the chief abbots of each sect, being their offspring, came to be revered enthusiastically by the believers, whereas in the West the worship of the descendants of LUTHER or CALVIN did not take place. This seems to be due to the difference in social structure between East and West. That is, in the modern West the tendency to esteem the lineage of a person almost ceased to exist, whereas in India or Japan of the corresponding period this attitude still remained.

In the Tokugawa period, SUZUKI Shōsan, who claimed to be the first Buddhist teacher to advocate lay Buddhism, discouraged people from taking holy orders and thus forsaking their vocations in the world. Tenkei would not differentiate clergy from laity.[111] The author of *Saruhōgo* took the same point. "When one engages himself in commerce with the spirit of compassion and equality, it is enlightenment, the goal of the Way. When one is thus right and intelligent today, there is no need of being apprehensive of tomorrow. So, if one lives right in this life, one should not worry about the future life."[112] However, the abolition of the distinction between clergy and laity was not actually realized, probably due to social pressure by the Government.

Although we cannot hastely conclude that the layistic tendency is common to all modern religions, we may safely say that it appeared rather early in the modern ages throughout many countries in both East and West, developed later, and is now conspicuous in many modern religions.

Approach to the Common People

The attitude of esteeming man himself led thinkers to a more affectionate view of the common people. They wanted to keep in close touch with the common people.

In Japan of the thirteenth century religious leaders began to employ Japanese in place of Chinese to expound their teachings in writings. Up to that time Chinese had been the formal language for the purpose. Especially in the Tokugawa period many Buddhist works written in easy, understandable Japanese were published for the common people. Like LUTHER, Shinran composed hymns intended for use at divine service in praise of the redemption which follows upon grace. In the conduct of worship he assigned an important place to the sermon.

In the Mediaeval West logical works were written in Latin alone. Antoine ARNOULD, together with Pierre NOCOLE compiled *La Logique de Port-Royal* in French for the first time in 1660. In ancient and mediaeval Japan all the works on Buddhist logic were written in classical Chinese. It was Echō Chikū (1780–1862) that wrote a logical work in Japanese, which was entitled *Immyō Inu Sanshi* (Buddhist Syllogism in Imitation of Masters' Works). However, the author claimed the work to be a mere imitation of authoritative works. Here we find a problem in the fact that no attitude of protest against the tradition was displayed and that progressive scholarship was not carried on with confidence, but with humility.

What made a difference in popularization of knowledge through writings between West and East was a difference in typographycal technique between the two. In the West the invention of the printing machine made it easy to spread knowledge, while in China and Japan wood-block print was used, which helped to a great extent.

Service to People

A movement which denounces religious bigotry and rites and asserts the significance of love and activity in social life, tends to encourage service to people. Among some thinkers devotion to God took the form of love for humanity. The spirit of service to mankind, even including those to come in the future, was enhanced in the modern ages.

Parallel to the increase of humanitarian activities in the modern West, we find a similar move in Eastern countries as well. In Japan of this period, some unique features can be seen in the expression of humanitarian attitude, which was displayed even in warfares. To the mountain-locked province of his enemy, UESUGI Kenshin (1530–1578), a feudal lord, sent salt in 1542 A.D., not to have the people of his enemy's province suffer from lack of salt.[113] The captives of the Korean Campaigns (1592–1598) were treated in a brotherly manner in Japan and were sent home safely.[114] After the Roman Catholic rebellion in Shimabara (1637) was quelled, religious ceremonies were conducted and three big monuments were erected, not in the memory of the victory, but for the spiritual repose and beatitude of the Catholic converts killed in the rebellion,[115] who were pagans in the eyes of the Japanese. This humanitarian act may have been due to the Buddhist ideal. At any rate the attitude assumed by the Japanese on such an occasion seems to have been quite different from that in the Mediaeval West.

In Japan the spirit of solidarity was greatly emphasized and mutual aid was practised among the people. Individual Buddhist priests engaged themselves in humanitarian activities, such as the distribution of rice and money to the poor and of medicines to the sick.[116] Their activities ranges over healing the sick, constructing bridges, instituting public baths and many other social works. For example, Tetsugen (1630–1682)[117] raised funds to save the lives of starving people in the years of bad harvests. Ryōō (1630–1707) established dispensaries and some 70 libraries in various cities. St. Mokujiki dissuaded feudal lords from engaging in battles, to save people from suffering.[118] But activities of this kind were not duly organized. In fact there were few organizations for this purpose, and if any, their existence was only temporary. The traditional solid family system and the spirit of solidarity among the people seemed to have lessened the necessity of organized humanitarian activities.

As an outstanding figure in the attitude of rendering service to others, we can mention NINOMIYA Sontoku. The teaching of morality and rendering help to others was combined by Sontoku with economic measures, such as a scheme for the rotation of crops, an organization for the circulation of capital, and accumulation of funds for famine relief.

Thus Sontoku viewed human life as a process of co-operation and mutual helpfulness and this combination of moral ideas and economic measures is the embodiment of his view. His influence produced practical effects among the peasants.[119]

Among Japanese priests there were some who engaged in the cultivation of land. Jōin[120] who was a Shinshū priest,[121] converted hundreds of acres of waste land into fertile paddy.

This event may not be worth mentioning but his record of cultivation displays interesting traits of modern thoughts. "It is true that a mere accumulation of riches is meaningless. But it is an act of delinquency to assume the attitude of believing indiscriminately in causes in previous existences according to the teaching of Buddhism, or believing in the mandate of Heaven according to Confucianism, or to 'waiting good fortune lying in bed' according to a popular proverb. If such an attitude is approved, the affairs of the world will be neglected, people don't give regard to expenses for luxuries, don't observe thirftiness, then they would get less clothing in cold weather and less diet in sunny days." Here a Buddhist priest is rejecting the conventional application of the traditional teaching of *Karman* to daily conduct.[122] "I want to cultivate the waste land granted by our feudal lord, and to leave the merit of my labour to our descendants. . . . Merely to inculcate people and bestow beatitude n the after-life cannot be called the way to save people. Buddhas and Bodhisattvas bestow benefits in the present life as well as in the future life."[123] However, this was an exceptional case, and generally speaking, economic activities were not closely related to Buddhism in this period.

The sympathy with the wretched common people led to severe criticism of the existing feudal system. ANDŌ Shōeki said: "Rulers, supported by their warriors, devoured the cereals which were the product of the direct cultivation of the masses, and, when the masses were stout enough to resist their tyranny, they gathered together the power of warrior class to oppress them and to punish those who had disobeyed the sage's order, fearing the charge that they were usurping the world of Nature. . . . The multitude of the warriors under those rulers eat without cultivating, and since there is a shortage of cultivators, the world inevitably becomes agitated and threatening."[124] This thought seems not to have developed into a public opinion or a sort of social movement in the period under discussion, but it is unnegligible as a step toward the development of modern thought.

Esteem of Ethical Values as over against Magic and Mysticism

A high esteem of man himself naturally leads to high esteem of ethical norms. As ethical values replace magical, ecstatical, or fantastic elements and hold an extremely important place in religion, the need to improve forms of religion as activity becomes imminent. This feature occurred in Japan as well as in the West.

In Japan the ethical character of religion was highlighted by some Buddhists of new type. Master Jiun advocated the "Way to become a True Man." He found the essence of Buddhism in the practice of the Ten Virtues (Good Vows), as opposed to the tradition of ritualistic Buddhism. He says: "Man's Path (or duty) by which a man becomes a (true) man consists in the observance of the ten virtues."[125] The Ten Virtues consists of (1) Not Killing, (2) Not Stealing, (3) Not Committing Adultery, (4) Not Lying, (5) Not Talking Frivolously, (6) Not Slandering, (7) Not Being Double-tongued, (8) Not Coveting, (9) Not being Angry, and (10) Not Being Heretical.

Master Jiun raised an objection to those many traditional priests who were preoccupied with the idea that these vows are only rudimentary steps to religion, and that the essence of Buddhism lies in elaborate rituals and esoteric doctrines. Jiun said: "Shallow scholars think that this moral is only for the laity (Sekenkai) and of small importance, that the moral for the monks who practise for their own merits (Shōmon, sravaka) is still imperfect, and that the moral for the Bodhisattva alone is high and noble. As a matter of fact this opinion has its origin in the false ideas that arise from attaching too much importance to names (or titles). This moral of the Ten Virtues is very profound and magnificent to anybody."[126]

Jiun coincides with modern Western thinkers in the assertion that religion should be realized in the practice of moral. But they stand on quite different standpoints when it comes to the concept of 'good and evil.' "Conduct which is carried out in conformity with the principle of reason (ri) in its relation to the three bodily, the four lingual, and the three intellectual (mental) activities constitutes the Ten Virtues, while the ten vices result from conduct contrary to the principle of reason. The obedience to reason is to stay in perfect harmony with nature and never mars nature either by increasing or by decreasing it. The obedience to reason is the maintaining of nature in equilibrium. When the original nature (honsei or honshō) is modified or perverted by the self-ness (shii) the ten vices are the result. The actions of body, of speech and of thought that are conducted without the interference of this self-ness are called the Ten Virtues. Although Buddhism *does not worry about the distinction between good and evil*,[127] goodness or virtue is always in accord with the nature of Buddha (busshō), while vice is non-accordant with it."[128]

NINOMIYA Sontoku, who also advocated the life of activity, had a similar conception of morals. Of good and evil he says: "It is men that bring about the idea of good and evil and the difference between them. There would be neither good nor evil without men. Man thinks it good to develop waste lands, and bad to neglect them, while the bear and the deer think waste lands good. The thief thinks it good to steal, but the law pronounces it an evil. We cannot discern what is good and what is evil. It is like saying near and far. Suppose you put up with two stakes apart, one marked with 'far' and the other marked with 'near,' it is not the stakes themselves but your position that decides which is really far and which is really near."[129]

Banjin, a Sōtō Zen master, said that the practice of Zen can be located in the observance of Disciplines. Hakuin denounced the custom of keeping concubines among the higher classes. Bankei admitted that women are more virtuous than men in many cases.

The attitude of emphasizing morals was very conspicuous among Zen masters who were often blamed for being indifferent to moral distinctions.

Conclusion

The number of original thinkers with traces of modern thought in Japan before the introduction of Western civilization was much smaller than in the modern West. My intensive trial was to find thinkers of this type, and yet I have not been successful so far. Even highly educated Japanese might come across unfamiliar names among those whom I have mentioned in this article. This fact means that indications of modern thoughts appeared in Japan only sporadically, did not develop, and vanished in their incipient stages. This phenomenon poses a big problem and needs further thorough investigation.

The discussion so far has pointed out and introduced, topic by topic, some features of modern thought which are worthy of study in comparison with modern thought in the West. We do not mean that all thinkers of modern Japan assumed the progressive attitude as remarked in this article. On the contrary there were many more backward or conservative, religionists than progressive reformers; they rigorously stuck to traditional or mediaeval ways of thinking and behaviour. Moreover, it is doubtlessly true that even progressive reformers themselves betrayed the conservative attitude in many respects without knowing it. However, the point we cannot neglect is the significance of the fact that the above-mentioned features were sprouting among those reformers. For so many traces of change for the modernization resulted from and centered around their attitude of esteeming the value of man as such in preference to anything else. It is also noteworthy that these thinkers of modern Japan were not militant theologians like LUTHER, ZWINGLE, and CALVIN. They could not completely upset the traditional organizations the establishment of which dated in ancient days, nor reform political and deep-rooted social systems. The attempts of these reformers produced no overwhelming influence upon the nation as a whole.

Although I have pointed out many common features to modern thoughts both in Japan and in the West, you will still notice that some features conspicuous in the modern West cannot be found in Japan of the same period. One of them is the idea of evolution. It is true that some Japanese thinkers had the idea of change or development very conspicuously in this period, but they never came to entertain the idea of evolution *i. e.,* the idea that something that comes later is superior to what is already in existence, and eventually replaces it. This idea of evolution was lacking in Hinduism, Buddhism, and Confucianism and other Eastern religions. You will all be able to think of cases that exemplify this.

Another feature of great importance is that the spirit of experimentation was almost lacking in Eastern countries of the same period. In Japan natural science did not develop; many new attempts were killed in their incipient stages by the pressure of the feudal governments. Mahayana Buddhism, a sect of Buddhism combined with Shintoism, posed no opposition to the appearance of innovatory trials, because its standpoint is flexible with regard to dogma, and found no contradiction to scientific attempts, whereas the feudal aristocracy tried to eliminate new attempts. Once the feudal system was destroyed, in countries where there was some opposition to science in one way or another by existing religions, it took some time to change people's attitude.

The features which I mentioned as already existing in Japanese tradition were representative of minority groups. Political and religious authorities ignored them, or occasionally suppressed them. It was only after the infiltration of Western civilization that they began to exert considerable influence in different ways, always, however, modified by the existing traditions.

1 Mo-ho-chi-kuan 摩訶止観, vol. 4b, in *Taishō Tripitaka,* vol. 46, p. 45b.

2 ISHIDA Baigan, *Seiri Mondō* 性理問答 (Dialogue on Human Nature and Natural Order). Translation, Introduction and Notes by Paolo BEONIO-BROCCHIERI, Roma, Istituto per il Medio ed Estremo Oriente, 1961, p. 13.

3 KAGAMISHIMA Genryu 鏡島元隆, *Dōgen Zenji to sono Monryū* 道元禅師とその門流 (Zen Master Dōgen and His Followers), Tokyo, Seishin-shobō, 1961, p. 112.

4 Ibid., pp. 106, 108.

5 Ibid., pp. 120, 124.

6 *Seiri Mondō,* p. 57.

7 Ibid., p. 57.

8 Hakuin's *Yasen Kanna.*

9 Robert Cornell ARMSTRONG, "NINOMIYA Sontoku, the Peasant Sage." *The Transactions of the Asiatic Society of Japan,* vol. XXXVIII, Pt. 2, Yokohama and Tokyo, 1910, p. 19.

10 This legend is not mentioned in the Pali four Nikāyas, but in the later works such as Buddha-biographies.

11 Japanese materialism in the Tokugawa period and after the Meiji Restoration is discussed in SAIGUSA Hiroto 三枝博音, *Nihon no Yuibutsuronsha* 日本の唯物論者 (Materialists of Japan), Tokyo, Eihō-sha, 1956.

12 E. H. NORMAN, "Andō Shōeki and the Anatomy of Japanese Feudalism" *The Transactions of the Asiatic Society of Japan,* Third Series, vol. II, Tokyo, Asiatic Society of Japan, 1949.

13 Shōbōgenzō 正法眼藏, chapter 25, Jinzū 神通.

14 SUZUKI Shōsan, *Ha-kirishitan* 破吉利支丹 (Refutation of Christianity).

15 H. DUMOULIN, YOSHIDA Shōin. *Ein Beitrag zum Verstandnis der geistigen Quellen der Meijierneuerung, Monumenta Nipponica,* vol. 1, Pt. 2, 1938, pp. 73–76.

16 R. C. ARMSTRONG, p. 18.

17 R. C. ARMSTRONG, p. 19.

18 Asō Isoji: *Takizawa Bakin,* Tokyo, 1943, p. 297.
(Another English translation of the NINOMIYA's poem:
No sound, no scent,
Yet Heaven and Earth
Proclaim at all times
The unwritten Laws of the Infinite.)

19 *Analects* 論語, IV, 15.

20 *Jishōki* 自性記.

21 *Jūzen Hōgo* 十善法語 (The Ten Buddhism Virtues. A sermon preached in 1773 by KATSURAGI Jiun), *The Transactions of the Asiatic Society of Japan*, vol. 33, Yokohama and Tokyo, Pt. 2, p. 44.

22 Ibid., p. 55.

23 赤心.

24 大義.

25 KATŌ Genchi, The Shinto Studies of Jiun, the Buddhist Priest and MOTOORI, the Shinto Savant, *Monumenta Nipponica*, vol. 1, 1938, Pt. 2, 9–24.

26 *Shinju Gūdan* (神儒偶談.)

27 KATŌ Genchi, op. cit., p. 21.

28 *Jūzen Hōgō*, p. 55.

29 *Seiri Mondō*, p. 26.

30 Ibid., p. 25.

31 Ibid., p. 29.

32 Ibid., p. 41.

33 Ibid., p. 43.

34 Ibid., p. 44.

35 Ibid., p. 55.

36 Ibid., p. 56.

37 Ibid., p. 33.

38 Ibid., p. 60.

39 *Shitetsu* 詩轍, chapter VI. 物真に逢ものは，事一轍に出づると見たり. R. H. VAN GULICK, MIURA Baien on Indian and Dutch poetry, *Monumenta Nipponica*, vol. 1, 1938, pp. 173–177.

40 ANESAKI Masaharu 姉崎正治, *History of Japanese Religions*, London, Kegan Paul, 1930, pp. 302–303.

41 E. H. NORMAN, p. 159.

42 E. H. NORMAN, p. 146.

43 *Seiri Mondō* 19–20.

44 SAIGUSA H., *Miura Baien no Tetsugaku* (The Philosophy of Miura Baien), Tokyo, Daiichi-shobō, 1931, p. 132; also *ditto*, *Nihon no Yuibutsuronsha*, p. 93.

45 其達観する処の道は，則條理にて，條理の訣は反観合一. 捨心之所執. 依徴於正のみに候.

46 MIURA Baien's thought was discussed by Gino K. PIOVESANA, *Monumenta Nipponica*, vol. 20, Nos. 3–4, 1965, pp. 389–443. Cf. p. 402.

47 YANAGI *Muneyoshi Senshū* (Selected Works of YANAGI Muneyoshi), vol. 9, Tokyo, Shunjū-sha, 1955.

48 KATŌ Genchi, *Shinto's Terra Incognita to be Explored Yet* (for private circulation), Gotemba, Japan, 1958, pp. 13–14.

49 *Jingū Hiden Mondō*, cited in KATŌ.

50 *Roankyo* pt. 1, in *Zemmon Hōgo-shū* 禅門法語集

51 *Munan Zenshi Kanahōgo* 無難禅師假名法語 in Zemmon Hōgo-shū

52 E. H. Norman, op. 315

53 *Jishōki*

54 KAGAMISHIMA G., p. 116 and 22.

55 FURUTA Shōkin 古田紹欽, *Kinsei no Zensha-tachi* 近世の禅者達 (Zen Buddhists in Modern Japan), Kyōto, Heirakuji-shoten, 1956, pp. 126–135.

56 *Jishōki.*

57 Joseph SOAE, *Monumenta Nipponica,* vol. 5, 1942, p. 182, No. 1.

58 YANAGI M., vol. 9, p. 321.

59 *Seiri Mondō,* p. 54.

60 Ibid., p. 55.

61 IWAHASHI Junsei, *Sorai Kenkyū* (Studies on Ogyū Sorai), Tokyo, Seki-shoin, 1934, p. 433.

62 *Keizairoku,* vol. 1, fol. 10.

63 *Seigaku Mondō,* 3, quoted in *"Nihon Kogakuha no Tetsugaku"* (Philosophy in Japanese Classical Study Group), by INOUE Tetsujirō, Tokyo, Fuzambo, 1921, p. 693.

64 *Seigaku Mondō,* quoted by INOUE T.

65 Alicia Orloff MATSUNAGA, *Monumenta Nipponica,* vol. 21, Nos. 1–2, 1966, pp. 203–209. Cf. NAKAMURA Hajime, *Ways of Thinking of Eastern Peoples.*

66 *Tamakatsuma* 玉勝閒, p. 693.

67 古事記傳 *Kojiki-den,* I.

68 *Kodō Taii* 古道大意, vol. 2, in *Hirata Atsutane Zenshū* (Complete Works of HIRATA Atsutane), by UEDA Mannen, ed., vol. 7, Tokyo, Naigai-shoseki, 1932, p. 69.

69 *Kōdōkwanki* 弘道館記 (A Prologue for Founding the Kōdō Institute), translated by KATŌ Genchi, Tokyo, Meiji Seitoku Kinen Gakkai, 1937.

70 *Seiri Mondō,* pp. 42–43.

71 *Byōsha Bō-koji ni Shimesu* (A Letter to a Certain Sick Layman).

72 *Jūzen Hōgo,* p. 34.

73 To Illustrate: In a monastery headed by master Bankei there was a monk who committed theft. He knew it, but he protected him not to be punished. (See, *Bankei Zenji Goroku* 盤珪禅師語録, Iwanami-Bunko-text, p. 234).

74 專人倫.

75 PIOVESANA, op. cit., pp. 417–418.

76 *Seiri Mondō,* p. 51.

77 This tendency is especially discussed by MURAOKA Tsunetsugu. *Studies in Shinto Thought,* translated by Delmer M. BROWN and James T. ARAKI, Tokyo, Japanese National Commission for UNESCO, 1964, pp. 95–170.

78 Cf. N. Skene SMITH, Tokugawa Japan as a Field for the Student of Social Organization, *Monumenta Nipponica,* vol. 1, 1938, pp. 165–172, especially, p. 170.

79 OGATA Dōken, "Kuden Hōmon no Jissen Rinri (The Practical Ethic of the Oral Tradition)," *Nippon Bukkyo,* No. 2, October, 1958, pp. 41–49.

80 *Jūzen Hōgo,* p. 53.

81 *Saru-hōgo* 猿法語, in *Zenmon Hōgo-shū,* vol. 2, p. 253.

82 *Munan Zenji Kana-hōgo,* p. 378.

83 *Roankyō,* Pt. 1.

84 *Jūzen Hōgo,* p. 48.

85 *Gomō Jigi,* vol. 1, fol. 3.

86 *Dōji mon* 童子問 (Questions by Children), vol. 2, p. 39.

87 IWAHASHI Junsei, *Sorai Kenkyū,* p. 449.

88 OGYŪ Sorai, *Rongo-chō* 論語徵 (Comments on the Analects of Confucius), cited in IWAHASHI, p. 300.

89 *Analects*, IX, p. 16.

90 *Seiri Mondō*, p. 57.

91 *Rongo Kogi* 論語古義, vol. 5, ch. YOSHIKAWA Kojiro 吉川幸次郎, *Shinajin no Koten to sono Seikatsu* 支那人の古典とその生活 (Chinese Classics and Life), Tokyo, Iwanami-shoten, 1944, p. 154.

92 HIYANE Yasusada, *Nihon Shūkyōshi* (History of Japanese Religion), p. 828.

93 *Kōdōkwanki*, pl. 10.

94 ANDŌ Shōeki, *Shizen Shin'eidō* 自然真営道 (The Way of Nature and Labour).

95 E. H. NORMAN, p. 299 ff.

96 E. H. NORMAN, p. 303 ff.

97 E. H. NORMAN, p. 305 ff., 315 ff.

98 R. C. ARMSTRONG, p. 9.

99 寄さし.

100 みこともちて.

101 NISHIDA Nagao, 西田長男 *Nihon Shūkyōshisō-shi no Kenkyū* 日本宗教思想史の研究 (Studies on the History of Religious Thoughts in Japan), Tokyo, Riso-sha, 1955, p. 178 ff.

102 *Ketsujō-shū* 結縄集.

103 *Roankyō*, last part.

104 Ibid., p. 337. *Banmin Tokuyō* in *Zenmon Hōgo-shū*, last part, p. 536 ff. R. N. BELLAH, *Tokugawa Religion. The Values of Pre-Industrial Japan*, Chicago, Free Press, 1961, p. 118.

105 ISHIBASHI T. und H. DUMOULIN, "Aus dem Kanon der Nyoraikyō" *Monumenta Nipponica*, vol. 1, 1938, pp. 222–241.

106 YOSHIMOTO Tadasu, *A Peasant Sage of Japan: The Life and Work of Ninomiya Sontoku*, translated from the *Hōtokuki*, London, Longmans, 1912, p. 223.

107 The Jesuit missionaries who came to Japan in the middle of the 16th century at once became aware of relationship between Jōdo-Shinshū-Buddhism and the "Lutheran heresy." Father Francesco Cabral reported on it in a letter dated 1571. (A. SCHWEITZER, *Indian Thought and its Development*, Boston, Beacon Press, 1957, p. 153) "Like Luther, Shinran rejected pilgrimages, excises in penance, fasting, superstition and all magical practices. He abolished the celibacy of the priesthood, of the monks and of the nuns. True piety was to be preserved in the family and in the worldly calling. He recommended to the laity the diligent study of the holy scriptures. And he demanded that the people should be delivered from their ignorance by good schools." (p. 152.) "Man is not in a position in any way to earn bliss by his own merits. In spite of this, Shinran required ethical conduct, and, be it noted, required it like Luther, as an expression and the fruit of faith in redemption." (p. 152.)

108 NAKAI Gendō, *Shinran and His Religion of Pure Faith*, Kyōto, The Shinshū Research Institute, 1937, p. 28.

109 NAKAI G. p. 28 ff.

110 Vallabha was believed to have been an embodiment of a portion of Krishna's essence. (Monier Monier-WILLIAMS, *Brahmanism and Hinduism*, 3rd, ed., London, John Murray, 1887, p. 134.)

111 KAGAMISHIMA G. p. 107.

112 *Zenmon Hōgo-shū*, vol. 2, p. 253.

113 TSUJI Zennosuke 辻善之助, *Nihonjin no Hakuai* 日本人の博愛 (The Humanitarian Ideas of the Japanese), Tokyo, Kinkodo, 1932, p. 97 ff.

114 Tsuji Z. p. 108 ff.

115 *Nihonjin no Hakuai.*

116 The details are mentioned in Tsuji Z., *Jizen Kyūsai Shiryō* (Works of Japanese Social Work), Tokyo, Kinkodō, 1932.

117 Tesugen's life is described in English in *The Light of Dharma*, August and October, 1901, San Francisco, pp. 22–25 and pp. 25–28. Also Washio Junkyō's 鷲尾順敬 article in the *Hansei Zasshi* 反省雑誌, vol. 12–13, 1897–1898.

118 Tsuji Z. *Nihonjin no Hakuai*, p. 346.

119 Anesaki M. p. 303.

120 Jōin, *Uyō Shūhoku Suido-roku* (Records of exploitation of North-Eastern Districts), 7 vols., in *Nihon Keizai Taiten* (Japanese Classical Works on Economics), vol. 30, edited by Takimoto Seiichi, Tokyo, 1929. This work was written in the Temmei period (1781–1788).

121 Ibid., p. 10.

122 *Uyō Shūhoku Suido-roku*, pp. 9–10.

123 Ibid., p. 11.

124 E. H. Norman, pp. 106–107.

125 *Jūzen Hōgo*, p. 1.

126 Ibid., p. 2.

127 "Zen'aku tomoni samatagenu."
Atkinson, the translator, did not translate this phrase which is highly Buddhistic. Probably, he, as a Christian missionary, found the phrase too strange.

128 *Jūzen Hōgo*, pp. 2–3.

129 R. C. Armstrong, op. cit.

CHAPTER VI

MODERN TRENDS—Specific Problems of the Tokugawa Period

1. Religion and Capitalism

The Problem

After the Meiji Restoration Japan tried to take in Western culture with great rapidity, but she still lacked sufficient understanding of the modern spirit which had been the motivating power in building up that culture. Recently there has been again a vigorous discussion about her inability to develop such modern spirit. In this connection I would like to consider the problem as to what relationship on earth religion has to capitalism in modern Japan.

If one looks at the modern history of this country, one can see the embryo of capitalism already in the Tokugawa period, but only it did not grow to the extent comparable with that in the West. In Japan, therefore, no civil society or the consciousness of citizenship could come into existence. Scholars have often made efforts to find out whether or not the various aspects of Western capitalism, at least in its early stages, owe their origin and development to the Protestant movement, especially to Calvinism. Max WEBER contends that the chief characteristics of the spirit which underlies the practical life of the Japanese have been determined not so much by religious elements as by another completely different factor, namely, the feudalistic nature of the social and political structure of society. It was precisely this feudalism that crushed foreign trade and obstructed the development of a civil society in the European sense of the word. He claims that the concept of a city possessing its own autonomous laws is completely foreign to Japanese thought.[1] After a study of the history of Japanese society and her various religious sects he makes the following criticism: "With the exception of the Jōdo Shin Sect,[2] the great majority of the religious sects led the laity to a form of worship that was irrational in the extreme and were far from educating them in a reasonable way of life. In fact the type of Buddhism existing among the laity simply developed a one-sided way of thinking—a conviction that the world (including human life and all things that pass) is valueless—together with an attitude of indifference towards secular society. And furthermore it spread abroad doctrines of retribution and magic as forms of escape."[3]

Jōdo Shin Sect is "a religion of worldly faith not bound by the self-reliant asceticism of the devotee,"[4] and yet even this sect did not develop "a rational asceticism for the laity." This is for the same reason as Lutheranism, for it is a religion of salvation which in medieval fashion dominated the mentality of the middle classes, it was not able to adopt the magic and the wild ecstasy that appealed to the masses in ancient Hinduism nor the strongly emotional devotion of later Hinduism and of Western pietism. The word "emotion" as used here means what might be better expressed by "feeling" (*kibun*).[5]

Max WEBER then draws the conclusion that in Japan, as in other Eastern countries, the spirit of capitalism did not develop. This proposition is widely accepted in Japan as a common knowledge of every educated person. But did the spirit of modern capitalism entirely fail to appear in Japanese religion? In my opinion one should not be too dogmatic in making such assertion.

The Problem in Tendai Sect

The question whether modern capitalism took its origin from the religious movement of Calvinism alone is difficult to answer. If, in this case, one does not take into account the contradictions inherent in the social and economic structure of Western society and their exposure and breakdown, together with such factors as the reform in production technique accompanying the progress in natural science and the enormous growth of circulating economic blocs based on the progress in communications—if one does not keep in mind all these considerations, one may reach the hasty conclusion that this phenomenon originated from one element alone. However, let us disregard the problem here. For the present purpose, suffice it to say that, though a great variety of social and economic circumstances are to be kept in mind, one can reasonably assert that Calvinism was a powerful spiritual force in building up modern capitalism.

But modern Japanese Buddhism, which held the position of the national religion before the Meiji Restoration, did not succeed in effecting any new economic movement. Rather it was completely cut off from the realities of economics. The Japanese bourgeoisie, even in its beginnings, did not associate economics with religion. Consequently, though Japanese Buddhism in the Middle Ages effected a general reform of ancient Buddhism in its so-called Kamakura form, it did not achieve anything to compare with the western Reformation. This is a fact of common knowledge.

However, if we examine the matter in detail, we find that there did exist an ethics of economics already in the medieval Buddhism of Japan. This is the *kuden hōmon* of mediaeval Tendai[6] in regard to the orthodox Tendai Sect existing from ancient times. According to this teaching, it is the merciful will of the Buddha that man should make use of all natural things ranging from the rays of the sun and the moon to the trees and grass on the earth. Grass and trees have no soul, but since they perform work which benefits man they are already Buddhas. Property helps us in doing altruistic deeds. Business, being economic activity, is a form of asceticism and a way to enlightenment. "The work of the peasant, the anvil of the blacksmith, the plane of the carpenter—all these are essentially expressions of Buddhist teachings. Consequently men's activities are regarded as entrances to the Doctrine" (Shūyōshō).[7] This document warns man, who is faithful to his employment and respects wealth, against injuring his soul and body and ending up in committing theft if he becomes poor. The work of farming aims at the autumn harvest. "If you can reap no harvest in autumn, everything is useless," it declares, thus underlining the importance of the fruits of labor. Emphasizing the necessity of saving, it asserts that, though one *sen* is a small amount, it will become a great amount if profit makes profit. If you are faithful to your work, it does not matter if you break the precepts by killing fish and fowl. Here appears a way of thinking that to be faithful to one's work is to follow the way of the Buddha.[8]

Suzuki Shōsan[9] *and the Ethics of Work*

(1) Fundamental Standpoint

At the very beginning of the modern era in Japan we can find an aspect of Buddhism which would have developed into the spirit of capitalism, if only it had developed. This is the ethics of work propounded by the Zen monk SUZUKI Shōsan and his school. I would like to examine the nature of his theory and at the same time enquire into the reasons why it failed to develop into a practical religious and economic movement.

SUZUKI Shōsan is a Buddhist whose name is almost unknown in the annals of Japanese Buddhism. If you look up books like *A History of Japanese Buddhism* and *A History of the Japanese Zen Sect,* you can hardly find his name. Even in various large Buddhist dictionaries his name is not listed. And yet in the Buddhism that he propounded we can find many modern elements that ought to claim our attention.

Shōsan belonged to a family of *bushi (samurai)*[10] in Mikawa Province (present Aichi Prefecture). He was born in the seventh year of Tenshō (1579) in Mikawa-no-kuni, Higashi-kamo-gun, Norisada-gō (Morioka Village) as the eldest son of a Matsudaira[11] vassal named SUZUKI. His popular name was Kyūdayū.[12] Shōsan was his secular name, though even after leaving the world he continued to use it. He participated in the battle of Sekigahara[13] and the summer and winter campaigns of Osaka and fought with great distinction. As a vassal of the Shōgun he was an important personage. In the sixth year of Genna[14] (1620), however, he quite suddenly abjured the world and became a monk at the age of forty-two. Before taking this step he had frequently lodged in Buddhist temples and had been on friendly terms with several famous Zen monks of his day. It seems that in the ceremony of *tokudo* the officiating monk was Daigu Oshō of the Rinzai Sect.[15] After this he made pilgrimages to various parts of the country, practicing asceticism. In the ninth year of Kan'ei (1632) he founded the Sekiheizan Onshin-ji Temple[16] in his native place. In the first year of Keian[17] (1648) at the old age of sixtynine he went all the way to Edo and engaged in educating the citizens. At the hour of the monkey (4 o'clock in the afternoon) on June 25th in the first year of Meireki[18] (1655) he died at Kanda in Edo.

The striking feature of his thought as a whole is the intensely critical spirit. First of all, he consistently took a very critical stand against the traditional Buddhist sects which had existed until his time. He himself belonged to the Sōtō Sect, but he used words of violent criticism against the sayings of Dōgen,[19] the founder of that sect, holding that Dōgen himself had not attained to the most profound enlightenment. Moreover, he did not recognize the authority of the founders of the various Japanese Buddhist sects and criticized famous Zen masters since the time of Chinese Buddhism one after another.

However, even though he did not recognize the authority of particular individuals or groups, he advocated a complete turning to the Buddha heart and soul. "Imagine that the Buddha is alive here and now, and worship Him with your whole being," he said. While radically denying the authority of past religious groups and the individuals who established them, he relied completely on self, and tried to come face to face with the Buddha.

His non-sectarian character was built upon such a standpoint. In general he devoted himself to the Sōtō Sect, but he had friendly relations with many teachers of the Rinzai Sect and was inclined to the thought of the Chinese Fuke.[20] Also he recommended the *nembutsu* to the general laity. He himself was ordained with the Novice Discipline by Discipline Master Genshun.[21] He was a complete liberalist. In fact he constantly used the word "freedom," saying that the aim of Buddhist asceticism was the practice of freedom. Of course, his "freedom" was religious and spiritual and not political or social, but when he insisted that the work of the businessman was "the freedom of the world" he used it nearly in the same sense as that of today. Thus aiming at freedom, he opposed various kinds of feudalistic ethics existing in his time and attempted at reformation—though it was of little avail. Among other Buddhists of the Tokugawa period there must be few who were so critical of feudalistic ethics as he was.

Another noteworthy expression of his critical spirit is found in his attack on Christianity, entitled *Yabure Kirishitan*[22] (An Argument against Christianity). While the Japanese of his day simply dismissed Christianity as *jahō*[23] (false teaching), sorcery and magic, he adopted a theoretical criticism of it. While the Buddhists of the time generally only sat idle when confronted with the problem of Christianity, Shōsan took up this problem and, not content with simply slandering and vilifying it, made a logical examination of its teaching. This fact points to his discernment as a thinker.

As a modern exponent of religion, he has left us numerous works, all of which are written only in simple, easily intelligible Japanese. In those days most Zen priests, whenever occasion offered, wrote poetry in Kambun (classical Chinese), but he entirely broke with this practice. Apart from him there was scarcely any Buddhist who wrote only in Japanese. Of course scholars of Japanese classics wrote only in Japanese. But unlike these people, he had not the slightest trace of pedantry in his writings. He was a man of the masses. One could point to many notable characteristics of this progressive thinker. Now I would like especially to examine his theory of the ethics of business.

(2) Virtue in All Walks of Life

The most striking feature of the thought of SUZUKI Shōsan is his contention that the way of Buddhahood consists simply in devoting oneself assiduously to the secular business of one's life. In order to make clear this idea he wrote his book entitled *Bammin Tokuyō*.[24] This book is generally acclaimed by his followers to be the greatest of his works. Among most Japanese Buddhists there was a strong inclination to think that the way of the Buddha consisted in separating oneself from the world, secluding oneself in mountains and woods and performing Zen meditation or in devoting oneself to the constant recital of the *nembutsu*. For example, even in the city there was a tendency to place the essential character of the life of a monk in separating himself from secular life and living in a monastery. While the generality of lay people engaged in secular pursuits, they thought that the secular life and the life of faith were two different things. Suzuki Shōsan, however, acted against this viewpoint in vogue and tried to practice the way of the Buddha in the middle of the secular life.

"Buddhist asceticism expiates all sin and removes all suffering. This spirit is the secret of ease of mind and body, and applies to any person whether he be warrior, farmer, artisan or tradesman."

In his opinion, any kind of business was a way of Buddhist asceticism and by means of it anyone could attain to Buddhahood.

"Every profession is a Buddhist exercise. You should attain to Buddhahood through your work. There is no work that is not a Buddhist exercise. You can see this from the fact that every work contributes to the welfare of the world. Man is made in the image of Buddha and is endowed with the Buddha nature. He should never commit the folly of turning aside to the way of evil."

According to him, all occupations were manifestations of the Absolute Being and had their respective social meanings. All occupations, superior and inferior, are holy as they are expressions of the unique and ultimate Buddha.

"The One and Absolute Buddha benefits the world, making his appearance in millions of beings. But for the smith, the carpenter and every other workman, we could not be provided with the necessities of life. Without the warrior we could not enjoy peace in our country. Without the farmer the world would lack its food. Without the merchant there would not be freedom in the world. There are various other kinds of occupations and everyone of them has some contribution to make to the world. Some investigate things about the heaven and the earth, while others examine the five viscera of the human body and practice medicine. Thus there is an infinite variety of callings, and all of them are of great service to the world. You must realize, however, that all this is the function of the One Buddha.

However, people of the world were not familiar with this reasoning. They felt that business life itself would contaminate and defile them.

"We are endowed with this blessed Buddha nature, but some people do not realize this and disgrace themselves, indulging in evil deeds and turning aside into the path of evil. All such people rightly deserve the name of common mortals full of illusion.

But he insists that each person must rely upon self with the conviction that he is a Buddha, because all living creatures without exception are, in the last analysis, united with the Buddha.

"All the Buddhas of the three temporal worlds have shown us by their very existence that all human beings are Buddhas. We distinguish colors with the eye, hear sounds with the ear, smell with the nose and speak with the mouth, and thus we have freedom to do what we want. But this freedom, whether it be freedom of the hand or the foot is to be attributed to the freedom of the One Buddha. Meanwhile the secret of salvation consists in faith in yourself. If you sincerely wish to attain to Buddhahood, you have only to believe in yourself, and according as your spirit becomes mature, you will naturally reach the supreme point of sincerity, finally getting confident and secure. It is then that you enter into unconsciously into the state where there exists neither self nor others and where you have no notion of space; and the true Buddha hidden in yourself manifests himself. Only have faith in Buddha; again, I say, have faith!

"The true Buddha hidden within yourself" or, in other words, your original self—to rely on this is the real essence of Buddhist teaching; and since any kind of business is an activity of this single Buddha, each person's devotion to his work can be made into a following of the Absolute. Accordingly, Buddhism since it aims at making a contribution to the world is the precious pearl of society. There can be no way of practicing Buddhism other than that of devotion to the worldly life of business.

"Buddhist scripture teaches us that we will certainly be delivered from worldly existence if we have passed through the way of the world.

The meaning of this is that *one attains Buddhahood by keeping the laws of the world.* Therefore the laws of the world are at the same time the laws of Buddha. As the *Avatamsaka Sūtra* teaches us, "The laws of Buddha are no different from those of the world; the laws of the world are no different from those of Buddha." You have not the least idea of the spirit of Buddhism if you will not listen to the truth that one can attain Buddhahood in keeping the laws of the world.

Basing his theories on this fundamental position, SUZUKI Shōsan maintains that, irrespective of the social and occupational distinctions which were beginning to be established in the feudalistic conditions of the Tokugawa period, each person should strive to put into practice the Buddhist teaching. In his *Bammin Tokuyō* he puts forward his own peculiar ethics of business, treating of warriors, farmers, artisans and merchants.

(3) Labor and Farming

In his *Bammin Tokuyō,* the chapter entitled "Daily Life of the Warrior" is followed by another in which he insists that the asceticism of the Buddhist way is automatically perfected by the farmer who devotes himself to agriculture:

"A farmer puts to me the following difficulty: It is very important to pray for happiness after death; but I am fully occupied with farm labor every day. While engaged in this lowly work I feel sad that I shall suffer in the world to come because of my useless life in this world. How can I arrive at the merit of Buddhahood?"

The way of thinking of this farmer is governed by the medieval assumption that religion is something precious, rising above the secular world, while business activity is something mean—"the lowly work of earning one's bread." In contrast to this, Shōsan thinks that devotion to agriculture is a way of Buddhist asceticism.

"Farming is nothing but a Buddhist exercise. If your intention is bad, farming is a lowly work; but if you are deeply religious, it is the saintly work of a Bodhisattva.

Whether farming is a way of Buddhist asceticism or not depends on the interior dispositions of the farmer who devotes himself to agriculture. Accordingly, in his opinion, the life of farming is no obstacle to the life of faith.

"You are mistaken if you long for leisure to pray for happiness in the next life. Those who have a firm resolution to attain Buddhahood lead an ascetic life. Those who pray for happiness in the next world, at the same time filling their minds with desire for pleasure, will never attain Buddhahood even if they keep praying through all eternity. Do hard work in the heat and in the cold; regard as an enemy your own flesh overgrown with evil passions; turn up the soil and reap in the harvest with your plough, your hoe and your sickle. Cultivate the fields with concentrated mind, as though you were doing penance. When you have time to spare, evil passions are apt to grow; when you are engaged in hard labor, sparing no pains whatever, you will never have your mind troubled with evil passions. Thus you can practice Buddhism unceasingly. Why should a farmer want to practice Buddhism outside of his work on the farm? Even the man who prepares to become a monk, devoting himself to pious worship, if he cannot get rid of selfish attachment, shall never be freed from the circle of transmigration, however laudable his achievements.

He attempts to see the religious aspect of the life of farming in the fact that this manual work entails much hardship. The medieval way of thinking that considers farming itself as something degrading was, in his opinion, utterly mistaken.

"If you make the great vow to expiate your sins through farming, and turn up the soil invoking the merciful name of Amida Buddha at each stroke of your plough, you will surely be rewarded with the fruit of Buddhahood."

From of old, manual work as a form of asceticism has been held in great esteem in the Western Church. But as HARNACK points out, reverence for work and its "authority" especially from the point of view of morality is not a characteristic feature of Christianity from the beginning nor is it its distinctive note. This point is especially emphasized by modern Puritanism which points the stream of Calvinism, and this is said to have an intimate connection with the establishment of modern capitalism. If it is true that all this is a peculiar feature of the modern (or at least the beginning of the modern) period, one can say that Shōsan's theory of work is equally modern.

After explaining the business ethics of farmers, Shōsan proceeds to that of artisans. The word "artisans" as used here corresponds to *kō* of the four grades *shi-nō-kō-shō*[25] (military, agricultural, industrial and mercantile classes). Here, asked the same questions by artisans, he gives them the same answers.

(4) The Ethics of Merchants

Shōsan finally treats of the ethics of merchants: *The Daily Work of Merchants*. And here he speaks to merchants in the same way as he speaks to farmers and artisans.

"A merchant puts the following question to me. 'Though I have been fortunate enough to receive the gift of life, engaged as I am in the humble way of trade, I am entirely preoccupied with the thought of gain. How sad that I cannot make efforts to attain enlightenment! Please show me how to attain to my end.'

As in the case of the farmer, the questioner is here taking the medieval point of view in regard to business. And in answer Shōsan teaches that the merchant must devote himself squarely to the acquisition of gain.

"My answer is this. Those engaged in trade should first of all learn how to make as much profit as possible.

Here the ethics of the pursuit of gain are openly stated. However, he stresses that the merchant must have great reverence for the virtue of honesty if he is to reap any advantage.

"And how can you bring this about? I suggest that you above all learn to walk the straight path of honesty, abandoning yourself to the way of Heaven. An honest man enjoys Heaven's blessing and is protected from disaster by Buddhas and deities. He naturally increases his wealth and is loved and respected by everyone. All will be well with him. On the other hand, a selfish person who pursues his own interest and devours gain at the sacrifice of others will incur the curse of Heaven and bring calamity on himself. He will be hated and despised by every-body. Everything will go wrong with him.

Because he is speaking as a religious man he uses concepts like "protected by Buddhas and deities" and "the curse of Heaven" in the course of his explanation, but if you take away these religious expressions it is almost identical with the reverence for, and emphasis on "honesty" made by the forerunners of modern capitalism beginning with Benjamin FRANK-LIN.

In general, he affirms the ethics of any social position and class existing in the feudalistic society of his day. He teaches that since one's social position, degree of wealth and length of life are all determined by "kar-ma," casting away one's personal interests and passions one should work for the good of the people.

"Whether your social status is high or low, whether you are rich or poor, whether you live a long life or a short one—all these things are predestined in accordance with the deeds practiced in your previous existence. It is useless to pray for fame or for gain; it will do you no good. On the contrary, you will only increase your guilt and be punished for going against the way of Heaven. Be in awe of this, and abandon self-interest. Regard your trade as a gift of Heaven and your-self as an agent who brings freedom all over the country. Leave your-self at the mercy of Heaven, cease to worry about gain, and be honest in business. Everything will go well with you then, for Heaven's re-ward corresponds to your deeds as naturally as fire burns things dry or water finds its own level.

He seems to recognize determinism, taking the standpoint that every-thing is fixed, but he attempts to put into practice the freedom of man. "Without the merchant there can be no peace in the world." Here, if you substitute "God" for "Heaven" and "the way of Heaven" and put "the salvation of God" in place of "freedom," can you not find in it the ethics of capitalism of the early period of modern Europe, tracing its foundation to Calvinism?

It is especially to be noted that in a vague way he is expressing the doctrine of utilitarianism. A man who had come down in the world said in the course of conversation: "I am content with poverty, and my heart is at ease." To this Shōsan made the critical answer: "Poverty is no good. It is better to be rich." He expressed this point of view when Buddhists and Confucianists were constantly advocating poverty.

However, he was by no means preaching materialism, much less was he advocating hedonism or epicureanism. He taught that even the man who made gain should not be attached to it. Following the general Buddhist viewpoint, he divides good into two classes: defiled good (one which contains attachment) and pure good (one which does not). The man who considers property to be something stable and clings to it, pursuing it as an end, looks for defiled good. But to be detached from personal desires and to be faithful to one's business on behalf of the people, reflecting that all things are impermanent—this is pure good. The merchant must aim at walking independently in the universe by learning this undefiled good. And this is the condition of Nirvana.

"You should not rejoice at good fortune. You must learn to distinguish what is called "merit with attachment" from what is called "merit without attachment." If you regard this illusory world of ephemeral beings as something substantial and eternal, doing good deeds with a strong attachment to life, such meritorious deeds are called merit with attachment. This merit with attachment is the cause of happiness and prosperity. However, if you become a rich man of high position through your merit with attachment, and enjoy a pleasant life, you will certainly come to the end of your fortune, and then you will have no choice but to degrade yourself in the ways of evil. This can be compared to an arrow shot into the sky, which falls to the ground when it has spent its force. Hence merit with attachment should not be entertained. But good without attachment is the source of enlightenment. Desire of Buddhahood occurs when you meditate on the truth that "All phenomena are transitory; all flesh is bound to die," and pay attention to the saying "There is no peace in this world; it is like a burning house." Good without attachment consists in praying for the divine bliss of Nirvana without any attachment whatever to the inconstant world of perpetual change. Therefore, you should make a vow to do good without attachment in your business of trade and increase your piety, keeping the truth in mind that everything in this world is ephemeral and subject to change. Sacrifice yourself for the world; purely for the sake of your country and your brothers, transmit the products of your district to another district and bring the products of other districts to your district, and convey them to the farthest land. Travel from place to place with a firm intention of promoting the welfare of the public, and realize clearly that your work itself is nothing but practice of Buddhistic discipline in expiation for your sins. You do penance when you go over mountains; you purify your soul when you cross rivers and streams; you learn self-renunciation and chant sūtras when you go sailing over the vast ocean. Reflect that life is only a journey through the transitory world. Cast off any attachment whatever and engage in trade without desire of gain, so that Heaven will protect you and various deities will benefit you. You will then become a man of good fortune yet you will disdain simply to remain a person of wealth. Your faith will become adamant in the end so that you will attain to the state of silent contemplation all the time no matter what you may be doing. In this way you will naturally attain enlightenment and taste the divine bliss of Nirvana. The result will be that you will get complete freedom from all obstacles and become independent of the universe. This everlasting joy has no comparison. Bear this carefully in mind, and observe it faithfully."

Here are developed the business ethics of Buddhism. Now "earnestly seek gain; but having attained to it, do not enjoy it; use it for the people"—these words of Shōsan teach us the following points from the economic point of view: 1) The pursuit of gain, 2) to save one's gain and not to use it as consumer's goods for pleasure, or, in other words, the accumulation of capital, and 3) to circulate capital advantageously. Accordingly, if one analyzes Shōsan's assertion from the economic point of view, the same way of thinking is at work as in the capitalistic ethics of the early period of the modern West. In the assertion that the merchants effect the freedom of the world and "get independent in the

universe," we can see the reflection of the thought of the merchant class
then on the rise. An attitude of restraint in regard to spending is an outstanding feature in the sermons of the monks of Jōdo Shin Sect to the
laity of the day, but this teaching was quite contrary to that of Shōsan
which I have quoted.[26] In the case of NINOMIYA Sontoku[27] this further
developed into the theory of capitalism.

(5) Religion in Business

In another of his writings, Shōsan refers to the vocational ethics of
monks, doctors, artisans and hunters. Here I am only attempting to
introduce his thought in outline. In the history of Japanese Buddhism
he was probably the first to develop an ethics of business on such a large
scale.

In Japan, the phrase from a chapter of the Lotus Sūtra which reads,
"Any occupation to earn one's livelihood is not inconsistent with Absolute Truth" was much in vogue until then, but this is satisfied with the
teaching that there is no contradiction between Buddhism and the secular
life. It is beyond dispute that Jōdo Shin Sect, adopting the position of a
secular Buddhism, devoted itself to the task of building the life of faith
upon the life of business, but in its mode of expression it does not escape
from the notion that the secular life is something defiled and of little
value. Rennyo[28] also teaches: "Now in my belief one ought not simply
to endeavor to subdue the evil thoughts and distracting illusions that
occur in the mind. You are free to engage in trade, or to serve your
master, or to become a hunter or a fisherman. You have only to trust
Amida Buddha firmly whose Original Vow is to save all the despicable
creatures like ourselves who are occupied day in day out only in these
lowly and sinful actions." But here the secular life of business consists
of "lowly and sinful actions." The medieval viewpoint of business has
not passed away. On the other hand, the assertions of Shōsan are much
more positive, for in this opinion the secular life of business is far from
contradicting Buddhism but is Buddhism itself.

SUZUKI Shōsan himself believed that he was the first in the history of

Japanese Buddhism to proclaim that the essence of Buddhism is the actual practice of business morality.

"From ancient times there have been many wise monks. Yet they were conversant only with Buddhist doctrines. No one has ever advocated that the laws of the world are applicable to everything. It is possible that such persons existed, but I have never yet heard of them. I assume that I am the first to profess this."

Although leading the life of one who had rejected the world, he continued to use his secular name "SUZUKI Shōsan" or "The old man SUZUKI Shōsan" when he published his writings.

In this way Shōsan respected secular Buddhism more than monastic one and tried to advise people against their desire to shave their heads and leave the life. While Buddhists in those days generally held that the monk should practice the way of asceticism confined to his room and the layman come to the doorway, Shōsan's contention was exactly the contrary.

Striving to practice Buddhism in the midst of secular life, he rejected the Buddhism of solitude, of mountains and of woods. Previously he had felt nostalgic for the life in the mountains and woods, but now he declared that this was not desirable. "I used to be fond of living in the mountains. The smallest wood was enough to tempt me to build myself a hermitage there. So I have often secluded myself in the mountains. But now I have to realize that this love of a secluded life comes from an ascetic temperament. This attitude is nothing different from that of the secular man who builds a garden or decorates a room."

To practice austerities in the midst of the mountains is not true Buddhist asceticism. They regard people in the world as the vulgar masses and simply build up their own self-complacent ego, "looking down snobbishly on the world." Faced by any chance of fortune, they fall with a crash. He teaches that a good example of it is the hermit Ikkaku who, after twenty years spent in asceticism in the mountains, was seduced by a woman. "It is better to practice Buddhist austerities in the world."

Consequently, Shōsan ended his days as a Buddhist of the city teaching, a form of Buddhism that was suitable for the people. Aiming as he did at a religion of secular life and of the people at large, Shōsan, though a Zen monk, ended up by rejecting *Zazen*[29] as a method of asceticism. He believed that it was wrong to exhaust the ascetic by making him practice assiduous *Zazen,* since the aim of Buddhist asceticism was to nourish the spirit. He was probably the first Zen monk publicly to dissuade people from practicing *Zazen.*

Now it could be argued that English Puritanism which is derived from Calvinism manifests the most thorough basis for the modern West's attitude toward business. According to Richard BAXTER who is one of the most representative figures of this faith, what is valuable for increasing the glory of God is not inaction or hedonism but action. Consequently, the waste of time is, in principle, the greatest sin, and inactive meditation (at least when it is practiced at the expense of business work) is valueless and, in some cases, should be completely rejected. In recent Japanese religion a contention exactly corresponding to it is made by Shōsan.

(6) Significance in the History of Thought

However, a theory like that of Shōsan was never accepted by the feudalistic society of his day.

"I have come through eighty years of hardship and none has ever listened to me. I am rejected by my contemporaries and am left to die and rot. In my sorrow I write this for posterity, hoping that there may be some prepared to read this even though there is no one who pays any attention to it today."[30]

This brings us up against the following problem: If Shōsan spoke in favor of secular Buddhism and preached reverence for action, why did he himself forsake the world? Is this not a contradiction? And to this he answers:

"I shaved my head simply because of my *karma.* Probably I was predestined to become a monk. It was of necessity that I got my head shaved."[31]

Here he adopts the standpoint of determinism.

It seems to me that we can find a solution to this problem in the following way. Shōsan, when he shaved his head and forsook the world, was sincerely seeking the Buddhist way. It was as a result of great experience that he finally came to stress secular Buddhism, but at this juncture it was already impossible for him to return to his former life in the world. In the centralized feudalistic society of the time, in which one's social position was regulated to the limit, even if a person who had left home and forsaken the world wanted to return to the secular life again, there was no possibility of his being accepted. Every profession was inherited, and it was especially difficult for a person of high position to return to the world. Therefore, Shōsan found himself in the contradictory position of disparaging the rejection of the world on one hand while leading a monastic life on the other. This situation he accepted as his *karma*. In the social structure of the time this fate was indeed a *karma*.

The notion that business is a holy thing and that its practice has a religious meaning is one held by the reformers at the outset of Protestantism in the West. It was already in evidence in LUTHER. At that time a terminology which speaks of business as a "calling" or "vocation" from God came into being. In the case of CALVIN this went so far as to be associated with determinism. On this point the ethical theory of business of Shōsan adopts the same stand. Each person's business is part of the One Buddha and is something bestowed by Heaven. However, all the leaders of Western Protestantism got married, had families and carried on the religious direction of people in the world as seculars. But Shōsan, though propounding secular Buddhism, maintained to the end the position of a monk. It is said that his followers consisted of fifty men, and they were all monks. It looks like a contradiction that he who attempted to prevent people from becoming monks should himself take monks as his disciples, but his biography shows that most of them first became monks under the direction of others and later turned to Shōsan and that it was only the rest of them that became monks in order to follow him. In either case, these people became monks of necessity in the feudalistic society because of some extraneous (especially social) circumstances. They felt subjectively that some karma from their previous existence had ripened ("the full development of virtue of a previous existence")[32] and so they became monks. Though he preached secular

Buddhism, the pressure of the feudalistic society of his day did not allow him to become a secular person.

In this way, although the ethical theories of the reformers in the West developed into a real force, those of Shōsan could not succeed in achieving an economic revolution in any concrete form. Max WEBER makes the excellent criticism that in the history of Japanese religion the State was not the protector of religion but was only the police for it. The powerful pressure of this police, which caused Japanese religion to decay, succeeded in utterly crushing a Buddhist movement in its embryonic condition, which, if only it had been able to develop into a real force, would have spurred capitalism to evolution.

2. The Science of Philosophies—TOMINAGA Nakamoto (1715–1746) and the History of Philosophies

Philological Method

It is widely believed that TOMINAGA Nakamoto (1715–1746) championed the "Mahāyāna Non-Buddhist" thesis upon reading a great deal of Buddhist scriptures. Admirers and refuters alike agreed to the effect that he read the entire Buddhist *Tripitaka*. Partly due to the extensive citations from numerous canons and partly due to his career as a proof reader at the printing office of *Tripitaka* at the Obakusan temple, this popular belief was well established. Appraisal of his works by the scholars of National Learning may have had the same function. MOTOORI Norinaga (1730–1817) wrote, "even the most well learned Buddhist priests would not excell Nakamoto in the amount of learning."[33] HIRATA Atsutane (1776–1843) supported it by saying, "Nakamoto with his fathomless learning read every scripture and every commentary of Buddhism."[34] But, upon the ground of careful collation of his citations with the sources he cited,[35] we are convinced that he did not read so many Buddhist scriptures either in the original language or in the Chinese translation. His learning of Buddhism has been overestimated.

That he did not read Buddhist scriptures as originated and recorded in India is verified as follows. Every sentence in Nakamoto's works starting with phrase, "such sūtra says so and so" is found in some commentaries written in Chinese.[36] Many of these citations correspond to the paraphrased citations of the commentaries made in China, but they often are missing in the text. Certainly some of his quotations are locatable in the original text and their Chinese translation, but these are found in some Chinese commentaries without being paraphrased. Besides, TOMINAGA Nakamoto misunderstood many Buddhist terminologies which he could have correctly understood only if he referred to the context of the texts. These examples indicate positively that he did not read the texts of Buddhist scriptures much.[37]

In spite of this undeniable technical defect, his honor as the prime philologist of this nation is not demeaned greatly. That he could formulate a historical and developmental structure of Buddhist philosophies out of the same materials that the tradition-bound Buddhist scholars made a poor use of is worthy of unlimited attention. The most noteworthy is that TOMINAGA Nakamoto, an eighteenth century merchant scholar lived in the commercial town of Osaka, framed a developmental history of Buddhist philosophies, while using exactly the same sources out of which the Buddhist scholars of T'ang China constructed an evaluative classification of Buddhist philosophies.

It was not the knowledge or materials but the way of handling the materials or the methodology of research that distinguished TOMINAGA Nakamoto from ordinary Buddhist scholars. It was nothing but the difference in the method that brought about a radically different result from the same materials. The philological method of study, which HIRATA Atsutane praised as a good approach,[38] awarded TOMINAGA Nakamoto an enduring eminence.

Humanism

A personal realization of the ethical principles oriented TOMINAGA Nakamoto to the philological methodology. In the philological studies, he did not commit himself to any traditional discipline, nor did he acquiesce to either Shinto, Buddhism, or Confucianism. He asserted that he was not a devotee of Confucianism, or Shinto, or Buddhism, but that he was a critical observer who maintained a personal viewpoint.[39]

Such was his basic position. Although several philologists were born before him in Japan, none of them ever went beyond the traditional framework of National Learning, Confucianism, or Buddhism. They were in want of the spirit of objective criticism. No one ever declared to be independent from the established doctrines. No one had enough philological ability to present a vital framework among the major philosophies in the context of their history and geography. TOMINAGA Nakamoto deserves the name who held the most extensive perspective among the scholars during Tokugawa Japan.

As TOMINAGA Nakamoto did not bind himself with any philosophical or religious school, there was no admitting "heresy" or "heterodoxy" for him. He could see the expressions of the human reason in what the Buddhist and other dogmatists regarded heretic. Rigid doctrinaire position of the Buddhists, for example, defined Brahmanism an abominable and evil heretic. TOMINAGA, however, said, "Who can prove it wrong when none of the critiques read so called Four Vedas and other literature of the tenet? The proponents of Brahmanism did not reach China, either. Then, if the Brahman teaching was correct or wrong was beyond the judgment for the Chinese critiques."[40] TOMINAGA also noted, in reference to the Mahakaccayana school that proclaimed the "being was void,"[41] and to the Chandaka school that advocated the "being in the negation of the void,"[42] that the evaluation of these philosophies by the Tendai philosophers and other scholars of the established doctrines was unduly low, and that it was lamentable. TOMINAGA was the one who rightly assessed the merit of these alien theses.

Thus, every thought, it seemed to TOMINAGA Nakamoto, was the equally valuable expressions of the human spirit. For him, the love of learning (philo-logia) was the way of life. Undoubtedly he was the prime philologist whom alone was this methodology truly realization.

This attitude made him unique among the contemporary philologists. MOTOORI Norinaga, the most distinguished National Learning philologist, did not attempt to evaluate the contribution of the Indian and Chinese cultures to the formation of the Japanese culture properly.

MOTOORI unequivocally rejected the value of the foreign cultures, while idealizing and applauding the ancient Japanese culture. MOTOORI's definition of learning was that it was the efforts to clarify the Ways of the Divine Antiquity. "Scholars must make it his duty to investigate and clarify the Ways of the Divine Antiquity. Scholars must not invent a new way. Scholars commit themselves in the consideration and examination of the Ways of the Old, inform the results to others, and keep them in written forms so that the authorities may avail themselves of these records for ruling when time will come five hundred or a thousand years later."[43]

Scholars of National Learning uncritically rejected Buddhism and Confucianism, and sticked to the attitude of subjecting themselves absolutely to the authority of National Learning. In spite of the fact that National Learning was a new discipline born during Tokugawa era, it consistently discouraged the students from criticizing their masters and encouraged them to devotional acquiescence to what their masters said. MOTOORI Norinaga's single-hearted veneration for KAMO Mabuchi (1697–1769) and HIRATA Atsutane's cathectic reverence in the authority of MOTOORI Norinaga support this comment. By this example is shown that they lacked the spirit of criticism. Scholars of National Learning were thus less realized to the essence of the love of learning than TOMINAGA Nakamoto, who studied Shinto historically and who attempted to systematize it. It was natural that TOMINAGA Nakamoto reproached the National Learning scholars on the ground that they neglected the historical development in Shinto. If we focus upon the degree of realization in the essence of philology as our standard of valuation, we have every reason to locate TOMINAGA Nakamoto above the scholars of National Learning.

Tokugawa Japan gave birth to some critical scholars from the Confucian camps also. ITŌ Jinsai (1627–1705) and OGYŪ Sorai (1666–1728) were leading such scholars. Their insight into the historical development of Chinese philosophies, however, was not as deep as NAKAMOTO, and they pursued the traditional method of research that had been customalized among the Sinologists. For these Confucianists, the Way of the Sages retained the absolute authority. Though critical in some measure, the studies of the Confucian classics as vanguard by OGYŪ Sorai yet found the supreme code of morality in the ancient ways of the Sages. OGYŪ Sorai wrote, "Whoever benefits others and saves people does good thing, because he does what many people would like to have them done. Of all good things, the way of the early kings is the best. Nothing is more valuable. The best way was stated in the way of the early kings."[44] The statement was the least coming for the position of TOMINAGA Nakamoto. "Recently Jinsai argued that MENCIUS alone inherited the proper philosophy of CONFUCIUS, and Sorai proclaimed that the Way of CONFUCIUS was identical with the way of the early kings, while CHU Hsi and MENCIUS misunderstood CONFUCIUS. These statements are drawn from the approach fundamentally mistaken."[45]

Among the Buddhist scholars of the day, Fujaku (1706–1781) and Kaijō (–1805) were distinguished in terms of the critical studies. That they were both Buddhist priests, however, turned out to be a limitation and restricted them from developing a scientific history of Buddhist thoughts. Fujaku went as far as doubting whether or not Mahāyāna was Non-Buddhistic, but this doubt ended in the attempt of verifying that Mahāyāna also was part of Buddha's teaching.[46] He explained that Mahāyāna was a secret teaching as against the overt teaching of Hinayana, and that thereby it was not known among the common followers. KEISHU Risshi was another champion of such thesis. KEISHU insisted that Buddha had secretly preached the Mahāyāna teaching only for a limited number of disciples, and that only such teachings that were open to the public were recorded as the teachings of Hinayana.[47] Kaijō proposed a hypothesis that the Buddhist scriptures were not necessarily the sermons that Buddha delivered in person, but that some of them were the expressions of enlightenment by those who received the insight from the teaching of Buddha. He presented a view that there must have been many compilers of the scriptures, even though their content should always express the thought of Buddha. Kaijō was thus very close to the "Mahāyāna Non-Buddhist" thesis.[48]

TOMINAGA Nakamoto was distinguished from these contemporary thinkers by the compassionate and sympathetic attitude open to any result of human effort. And he understood the human being aesthetically. TOMINAGA Nakamoto was an observer of the human phenomena, rather than an initiator of a social movement.[49]

Endemic Philosophy

By philological studies TOMINAGA Nakamoto attempted to understand the philosophies of different peoples in the context of the respective historical and endemic setting, and to clarify their mutual relationship.

TOMINAGA Nakamoto payed attention to the endemic conditioning of philosophies, and named it *Fūki*. The Indians' inclination toward mysticism, he said, was reducible to the Indian climate and geography. The reason why the Japanese did not develop an intricate mystical thinking was explained by the climate and geography of Japan quite different from those of India. Additional reference was made to a statement of a Chinese scholar who said that the southern people were agile because of the conditions of the area.[50] Although he did not discuss this topic exhaustively, what he had written contains enough to show us his proposition for the necessity of a science of the climate and geography.

The Way of Truth emphasized that the ethical principles were reflective of historical and endemic background. In the *Shutsujō Kōgo* (Historical Survey of Buddhism) TOMINAGA discussed that ethical philosophies ought to be considered in the context of the climatic and geographic conditions. He proclaimed that no philosophy could overcome the circumstantial and ethnic limitations in forming its characteristic. "Therefore in preaching or founding a way, the masters since the Divine Antiquity always made use of the local customs of the places where they would propagate the instructions. No matter how highbrow a way may be, it cannot escape this principle."[51]

TOMINAGA Nakamoto described the climatic and geographic reflections of the spiritual cultures of different nations with compact and appropriate phrases. Some of the illustrations follow.

According to him, Indian culture valued mysticism, Chinese culture valued rhetoric, and Japanese culture valued simplicity. "In terms of the discourse, the Indians favored limitless expressions, the Chinese liked impressive rhetoric, whereas the Japanese inclined to simple and straight-forward expressions."[52] The allegories of the Indians as "to put the Sumeru Mountain into a seed of opium," or of the Chinese as "flat mountains" or "the three ears of the elephant" were beyond the imagi-nation of the Japanese. These allegorical expressions, which were im-possible under natural circumstances, could work effectively and vividly only in so far as there existed literary traditions to support them. The Japanese, on the contrary, did not feel at home with these artificial ex-pressions. The statement that the Japanese used "simple and straight-forward"[53] expressions primarily was made by MIYOSHI Muneaki, a merchant from Osaka, and was perfectly agreeable to TOMINAGA Nakamoto. It is the most interesting that the intellectual merchants of Osaka in the 17th century held and brought into conversation such endemic considerations.

TOMINAGA Nakamoto claimed that the vice of the Chinese way of thinking was rhetoric. "The trait of the Confucian argument is the overabundance of rhetoric. Rhetoric is what we call oratory. China is a country which greatly delights in this. In the teaching of the Way and in the education of man, if one lacks proficiency in speech, he will find no one to believe in or follow him. For example, take the word Rites (ri). It originally signified simply the ceremonies on the four great occa-sions in life: coming of age, marriage, mourning, and religious festivals. But as you know they talk now of what is the Rite of a man as the son of his father, what is the Rite of a man as the subject of his sovereign. They speak of it in connection with human relationships. They speak of it in regard to seeing, hearing, speaking, and acting. They also assert that Rites owes its inception to the division of heaven and earth, and embraces the whole universe. Take another example, that of music (gaku). The character gaku originally meant to be entertained by the music of bell and drum. But then they began to say that music was not necessarily confined to bell and drum. Music, they said, was the harmony of heaven and earth. You can see the way they talk. Take again the character for sage (shēng) which originally signified a man of intelligence. They have gradually stretched it to the point where a sage is the highest type of

humanity, even capable of working miracles. Thus we know when Confucius talked of humanity, Tseng Tsu of humanity and righteousness,
Tsu Ssu of sincerity, Mencius of the Four Beginnings and the goodness
of human nature, Hsün Tzu of the badness of human nature, the *Book
of Filial Piety* of filial piety, and the *Great Learning* about [what the superior man] loves and hates, the *Book of Changes* about heaven and earth,
all of these are just ways of presenting the plainest and simplest things in
life with an oratorical florish in order to arouse interest and make people
follow them. Chinese rhetoric is like Indian magic, and neither of them
is particularly needed in Japan."[54]

The Indian spiritual characteristic was found in their dependence
on the magic. Teachers of India, therefore, had to employ magical expressions. "The Indian scholarship constitutes itself upon the magic.
Unless the scholarship is supported by miraculous stories, it does not
convince the students. The Indians are extremely found of the magic.
The magic for the Indians is like the rhetoric for the Chinese. In India
whoever preaches a religion or teaches an ethical doctrine must rely on
the magic. Whoever one may be, one cannot expect any follower if his
stories did not include miracles."[55] Therefore, Tominaga felt, it was only
natural for Buddhism that had emerged in India to employ for the purpose of communication the stories of the miraculous and wonderful
magics. "Other doctrines at the days of Gautama were unexceptionally
magical. When Gautama tried to overcome them by expounding his
own doctrine, he had no choice but showing superior magics." Thus it
turned out that the very bent toward the magic came to characterize
Buddhism.

"The vice of Buddhism is mysticism. Mysticism is what we call the
magic. India is a country which greatly delights in this. In the teaching
of the Way and in the education of man, if one lacks proficiency in
magic, he will find no one to believe in or follow him. Gautama practiced spiritual exercises in mountains for six years. It was solely for the
sake of learning the technic of getting into trance, and thus he became
good at getting into trance. The divine miracles and the divine powers
or knowledge described in various scriptures are expressions in terms of

magic. Phrases like 'representation of the universe in the white hair spun on the forehead of Buddha,' 'the strech of one's tongue that reached heaven,' 'Vimalakirti instituting eighty-four-thousand men in a room of ten feet square,' and 'the transfiguration of Sariputta into a woman' are a few of the magical expressions of Buddhism. Magic, then, was the most effective means of communication for the Indians, if they would explicate the causational principle and the existential meaning. Magic was thus a necessity for the Indians, but it is definitely unnecessary for the Japanese."[56]

The entire history of Buddhism appeared to be no more than the repetition of various forms of magical instructions. "When the disciples of Buddha forges theses, they present them as if they were Gautama's teaching. They do so in order to have them authorized by the name of Buddha. Theses in such guise are another type of magic.[57] Most descriptions in the Buddhist literature, therefore, are magic. "Nine out of ten teaching and commentaries in the three sections of the Buddhist scriptures are magic. . . . The most remarkable of the Buddhist scriptures is allegory accompanied with magic. Magic is commonly practiced in India and the Indians like magic."[58]

" 'Divine ability' is another form of Magic. It is the Buddhist term for what non-Buddhists would call magic.[59] The difference[60] is that non-Buddhists expect secular reward from it, while the Buddhists want to get it for the sake of spiritual exercise.[61] Whenever one reads Buddhist scriptures, one must be careful not to lose sight of the context by being dismayed by the unusual expressions. Readers must understand that the magical and miraculous stories are merely conventional measures of instruction. 'The principle of Retribution' that Buddhism teaches is another form of magic, and is not the truth of Buddhist teaching.[62] The traditional Buddhist scholars, TOMINAGA Nakamoto claimed, were not receptive enough to understand the endemic expressions of Buddhism. Therefore, the research of Buddhist doctrines, he urged, needed ample consideration of the ethnic peculiarities of India.[63]

A reference was made to Taoism which, unique among Chinese disciplines, favored magic like the Indians.[64]

To sum, "the vice of Buddhism was magic and the vice of Confucianism was rhetoric,"[65] and not very much were included in the Buddhist or Confucian teachings if magic and rhetoric were removed.[66] "Only if the Buddhist priests knew that Buddha expressed through magic and Confucius through rhetoric, they ought to realize that Buddhism and Confucianism were much simpler."[67]

What view did TOMINAGA Nakamoto hold as to Shinto and the Japanese way of thinking? According to TOMINAGA, Japan's ethno-endemic trait was, above all, the custom of "secret transmission," which was well represented in Shinto.

"The vice of Shinto is secrecy, devine secrets, and secret and private transmission, such that every thing is kept under the veil of secrecy. Hiding things leads to lying and theft. Magic and oratory are interesting to see or to listen to—they thus have some merit. But this vice of Shinto is of the lowest sort. In olden times people were simple, and so secrecy may have served certain educational purposes, but the world today is a corrupt world in which many people are addicted to lying and stealing, and it is a deplorable thing for Shinto teachers to act in such a way as to protect and preserve these evils."[68]

This characteristic was prevalent in every sphere of the daily life of the Japanese people.

"Even in such lowly things as Noh drama and the Tea Ceremony, we find them all imitating Shinto, devising method of secret transmission and authentication and attaching a fixed price to the transmission of these 'secrets' for selfish gain and benefit. It is truly lamentable. If you ask the reason why they devise such practices, their answer is that their students are immature and untried, and must not be granted to ready an access to their teachings. It sounds plausible, but any teaching which is kept secret and difficult of access, and then is imparted for price, can not be considered in accord with the Way of Truth."[69]

Thus TOMINAGA Nakamoto noted and rebuked the Japanese tradition of overestimating the lineage and of staying within the closed human relationship. TOMINAGA, born among the free merchants of Osaka, was a free thinker. He believed that this pre-modern characteristic of the Japanese people had to be amended.

Historical Relativism

TOMINAGA Nakamoto payed attention to the historical development of the philosophical traditions.

Whenever a philosophy was being formed, according to his discourse, it developed as a partial addition to the preceding philosophical basis while willing to overcome the predecessor. "Anyone who teaches a philosophy or founds a school of philosophy has a certain preceding authority upon which he relies. And he attempts to overcome it while comparing his thesis with it. It often happens that scholars of later years overlook the relationship between the predecessor and the latecomer."[70] In the history of philosophy, new theses appear consequentially.[71] "A new thesis is an addition to the existing theses."[72]

If such a frame of reference was taken, the students should come to consider the historical aspect of philosophy necessarily. Nakamoto denounced the traditional scholars on the ground that they little considered this feature of philosophy. This claim was revolutionary at the time of TOMINAGA Nakamoto, though students of humanities today may take it for granted. From this viewpoint, the religious geniuses of the old times were seen as the human who cumulated much knowledge through the years and who were bound with the past philosophies, if they attempted to transcend them. They were not the super-man whom the God gave special previleges. Now that religious heroes were the historical and the human beings.

In this thought is a humanist viewpoint comparable to the viewpoint of the modern western humanists. In the western hemisphere, humanism has existed not only in the modern times, but also in Classical Greece, Cicero being an example. What characterizes the modern humanism and was absent in Cicero is its growth through the struggle against Christianity and the Christian idea of life. Christianity, in fact, intervened the classical humanism and its modern renaissance.[73] In spirit TOMINAGA's historical study of Buddhist thoughts correspond exactly to the modern western humanism. It is his emphasis of historical observation that helped him organize a systematic history of Buddhist philosophies and that made him a distinguished figure among the Japanese philosophers.

In the research of the history of philosophies, TOMINAGA Nakamoto depended mostly on language analysis, holding a systematic opinion upon the nature of the discourse. Namely he proposed three "things" and five "categories" as criteria for textual criticism.

Three "things" were explained as follows. "My method of study emphasizes three things by which all human discourse can be properly understood. As long as one's approach is made through these three things, there is no discourse which defies clear understanding." Each of the three "things" was explained individually in detail.[74]

(1) "Discourse has man behind it." This meant that "as one man or one group of men differs from another, so does discourse." TOMINAGA illustrated this by showing how terminology employed in the various Buddhist scriptures reflected the different language and outlook of various authors. The terms thus specifically used by certain men or certain group of men showed their contention.

(2) "Discourse has time behind it." This meant that as each age had its own characteristics, so the pronunciation and spelling of discourse partook of it. TOMINAGA, showing that the different Chinese translations of Buddhist literature employed different rendering, explained that the same vocabulary was spelled and enunciated differently at different times. As the scholars by these days believed that the spelling and pronunciation of discourse were solid and immovable, this view sounded revolutionary at his time, though it is a common sense today. The accustomed use of the well established Chinese characters which survived the same symbol for a few thousand years had provided the scholars with the belief that the language was immovable. "Those who value the new translation claim that the old translation committed mistransliteration. But the fact is that the discourse and pronunciation differ at different times. They are different but both correct rendering from the sources of different times."

(3) "Discourse falls into different categories." These categories had particular reference to the ways in which different teachings or truths were further developed or modified in the hands of others.

a. Assertion or expansion, including exaggeration and metaphor.
This category was expressed in the character for the wave swelling up and luging forward. "Yuima-gyō (*Vimalakirti nirdesa sūtra*) says, 'Learning the law of universe is the academy.' Zenyo-kyō says, 'Natural departure from the craving is the academy.' These statements show the example of expansion or exaggeration. The academy is the academy, not identical with learning. Shintoists also make this sort of statement. For example, they say, 'The body of a man is the world in heaven.' In the mean time, Zo-ichi-agon-gyō (*Ekottarāgama, Tseng-i-a-han-ching*) and Kise-kyō speak of the four kinds of food. Only one of the four, *Dan-jiki,* is included in the ordinary concept of food. The rest, *Koraku-jiki,* implying clothes, houses, perfume, and furniture, *Nen-jiki,* implying thinking, imagination and conception, and *Shiki-jiki,* implying the matters which human eyes and ears recognize, are not ordinarily regarded as food, though the sūtra says they are. These, we must say, are the expansion of the discourse, 'food.' " *Jiki* originally meant the food edible by men through mouth only. Later other things came to be included in the word, which he called expansion. "People say metaphorically, 'to *eat* a hitting by a club,' or 'to *eat* a punch.' Dai-chido-ron (*Mahaprajnaparamitōpadesa, Ta-chih-tu-lun*) regards scriptures as the relics of the Buddha. But relics are relics. They are not written scriptures. These are examples of expansion. If scholars learn this, many questions become much simpler." These illustrations suggest us that TOMINAGA, with steady and scholastic perspective, attempted to investigate the truth behind the rhetorical exaggeration.

b. Generalization.
This category was expressed in the character for the wave spreading out. This category, it seems, referred to the general discourse, while covertly holding the particular reference behind the overt general ex-

pression. "The original meaning of Tathaga as applied to the Buddha was 'He who comes thus.' As the storehouse of the Mind, however, it was described in the Ryoga (*Lankavatara Sūtra*) as 'the source of good and evil,' and in the Hannya (*Prajna Paramita Sūtra*) 'All creatures from Heaven to Hell are embraced in the storehouse of the Tathagata.' " The expressions of this sort belonged to this category.

c. Collision or contradiction.

This category was expressed in the character for the wave breaking against the shore.[75] This seems to have implied such expressions that emphasized and extracted part of the general form of discourse. "It is said, in Shōman-gyō (*Srimālā-devi-simhanāda-sūtra, Sheng-man-ching*), 'The Buddha's Truth-body (*Dharmakaya*) does not exist apart from the world of passion,' and in the storehouse of Tathagata, 'The Tathagata is found amidst all the passions of the sentient world.' These are cases of collision."

d. Reversion or inversion.

This category was expressed in the character for the wave washing back. This was the case of using a discourse in the opposite of the original meaning. The Chinese expression "to follow one's own bent" as a translation for the Sanskrit *pravarana* was an example. "To follow one's own bent" originally had the bad connotation of lacking restraint; here it takes on the good one of acting spontaneously in accord with one's true nature."

e. Transformation or modification.

This category was expressed in the character for the wave turning away. This referred to the turning and elevating of the meaning of the original discourse. *Iccantika* in Sanskrit, for example, meant the most wicked villain without any help. Fa-Hsien, who traveled in central Asia, India and Ceylon between 399 and 414, said 'Everything has Buddha nature except *Iccantika*,' in the first translation of *Mahā-parinirvāna-sūtra, Nieh-p'an-ching*. Whereas the sūtra's later translation, known as *Ta-pan-heh-p'an-ching* described the comparable statement as, 'Even the *Iccantika* with no merit possesses the Buddha nature.' TOMINAGA stated, "I would believe that *Iccantika,* originally considered to be lacking a Buddha nature, should as a sentient creature capable of spiritual conversion possess the seed of Buddhahood, because the transformation or modification of the idea of potentiality for Buddhahood derives from the possession of spiritual self hood rather than from one's status among men."

When TOMINAGA proposed "Discourse has three things," his attention seems to have been paid the most heavily upon the personal particularity of the discourse. "As the frame of reference of my research, I say, discourse has three things. Different terms for a concept in different Buddhist scriptures reflect the different wording in the different schools or denominations of Buddhism. The unique wording of a school or a denomination is comparable to the trade mark of the merchants. Students of later years often forget the historical situation, and try to explain the terms independently and for their own sake, thus missing the links and the intentions of the original. This is the mistake in which later scholars often fall."[76]

Along with the process of diversification of Buddhist schools and denominations, every discourse attained many implications. The Chinese thought that "The diversity of meaning of the Sanskrit discourse cannot be compared to that of any other language," and they referred to the six different meanings for the word, *bhagavat.* But the vocabulary with diverse meanings was not the preoccupation of the Sanskrit. "The Chinese discourse contains many implications. Consult a dictionary, and you will notice many footnotes under every heading. They show the diversity of the Chinese discourse." TOMINAGA did not forget to mention that the Japanese discourse was not an exception. "Not only the Chinese, but the Japanese discourse implied many things."

TOMINAGA's study of the language has so far been covered. He explained his theses quite simply. We may have to mention that the theses were not clear enough in the present standard of philological criticism.

Yet it remains the most remarkable that he accomplished a synthetic and systematic philosophy of language with the historical perspective at the time when he lived.

The Way of Truth

TOMINAGA Nakamoto was the first who studied all the major philosophical systems of India, China, and Japan historically. A study of the history of philosophies or ethical thoughts is impossible without the student's own philosophical convictions. Without some ethical retrospection, a student can never systematize the ethical thoughts that appear before him. Then we ought to understand what the position accorded with his own conviction was, as long as we would expect a thorough understanding of his history of philosophies.

The ethical philosophy of TOMINAGA Nakamoto was presented in a book titled the *Okina no Fumi* (Testament of an Old Man). TOMINAGA claimed that he transcended Shinto, Confucianism, and Buddhism, and, upon synthesizing them, advocated what he calls the Way of Truth, or the Way of the Ways.[77] But if we analyze the teachings of the Way of Truth, we cannot find any revolutionary idea in them. The items of popular morality of his day constitute the Way.

"If you have a master, serve him well. If you have children, educate them well. If you have retainers, manage them well. If you have an elder brother, show him every respect. If you have a younger, show him every sympathy. Toward old people, be thoughtful; toward young people, be loving. Do not forget your ancestors. Be mindful of preserving harmony in your household. When associating with men, be completely sincere. Do not indulge in evil pleasures. Revere those who are superior, while not despising the ignorant. What you would not have done to yourself, do not do to others. Be not harsh; be not rash. Be not obstinate or stubborn. Be not demanding or impatient. Even when you are angry, do not go too far. When you are happy, be so within bounds. You may take pleasure in life, but do not indulge in sensuality. Be not lost in sorrow; whether you have enough or not, accept your lot as good fortune and be content with it. Things which you ought not take, even if they seem insignificant, do not take; when you ought to give, do not hesitate to do so even it means giving up all, even your country. As to the quality of your food and clothing, let it conform to your station in life and avoid extravagance. Do not be stingy, do not steal, do not lie. Do not lose yourself in lust, be temperate in drinking. Do not kill anything that does no harm to mankind. Be careful in the nourishment of your body; do not eat bad things; do not eat too much."[78] "In your free time study the arts of self-improvement; try to be better informed."[79] To sum, this was the way to teach to be virtuous.[80]

The Way of Truth was thus a concrete teaching by means of which men realized their ways in daily life. It was not an abstract concept. The way as the cause of human phenomena was "being done." If it was not realized in the world, it was not the way at all. The way was present in the phenomena of the world. It was not a product of imagination or thinking.

The world where the way functioned was composed of space and time. Therefore the way was necessarily bound by chronological and spatial limitations if it was to be realized in the world. Second characteristic of the Way of Truth was a derivative of the chronological limitation, namely, the Way ought to be in accord with the "present" necessities. Third was derived from the "spatial" limitation. The Way of Truth ought to be the way of "Japan." It was strongly held that the Way as the law of causality among the human beings was conditioned by the historical and endemic situations. The awareness of the importance of the historical and endemic elements in the human phenomena, if otherwise not much different, made the Way of Truth unique among the philosophies of the day.

Then the question was what the "virtue" was.

TOMINAGA simply explained that to do virtue was in accord with and to do evil was against the Way of Heaven, Earth, and Nature,[81] and did not deeply investigate the nature of the virtue. In the claim of doing virtue, TOMINAGA argued, the three established religions agreed completely.

"The way of CONFUCIUS and the way of Buddha are the same. Both demand to do virtue."[82]

The question was whether the teaching of the three religions and that of the Way of Truth were identical or not. Enumerating the items of virtuous and moral actions, TOMINAGA admitted that "All of these things are already mentioned in Confucian and Buddhist writings, and do not need to be made a special point of."[83] Then, why did he reject the three religions? Why did he champion the Way of Truth anew? Why did he distinguish the Way from the other ways?

He emphasized "the Way of Truth," primarily because it was the way "that is practicable in the present Japan."[84] This phrase illustrates the three concepts by means of which the Way of Truth was defined. Firstly, it ought to be practicable. "The phrase the way of the ways was derived from the fact of its being done. So the way which is not realizable is not the Way of Truth."[85]

Shinto, Confucianism, and Buddhism, or more precisely, Shinto as sponsored by the scholars of National Learning, Buddhism as explained by the contemporary priests, and Confucianism as lectured by Neo-Confucianists, were all "the ways ill approved by the Way of Truth," mainly because they neglected the historical and endemic traits of the human being. They were not the ways that should be practiced in Japan of the day. TOMINAGA pointed out how the customs and habits were different at different places and times.[86] Even the Buddhist priests and Confucian scholars in Japan could not rigorously observe the prescriptions of behavior as given in Buddhist or Confucian scriptures.[87] Imitation of the Indians or the Chinese was not only impossible, but meaningless.

The Buddhists' devotional adoration of the Indian culture, Nakamoto commented, was by no means plausible. "Buddhists learn the teaching of the Indians, attempt to practice the teaching, and dare to communicate the teaching to other Japanese. But none ever used nor any audience learned Sanskrit. Make a house and furnish it in the complete imitation of the Indian fashion, and you would learn it impractical. In India it is a good manner to reveal one's shoulder when saluting. Even the exhibition of one's thighs is an acceptable manner in India. There are ample such examples in the Buddhist literature. What should happen, then, if the Buddhists should imitate these alien habits?"[88] "Buddhist scriptures had it, 'Even if I should tell you something, you need not follow it in case it did not apply the custom of the place where you are. If my instruction do not cover what you want to know, do whatever is good at the place," and "Buddha did not teach for everybody to imitate the customs of India."[89] The true intention of Buddha in these words, TOMINAGA lamented, were not correctly understood by the contemporary Buddhists of Japan.

TOMINAGA Nakamoto insisted that the Confucianists' adoration of the Chinese culture was not practical either.

"In China meat is important food. If the Confucianists were to follow whatever ways CONFUCIUS had taken, they should store beef and mutton, and live on them, . . . They should converse in Chinese and use Chinese characters. Out of several variations, they should choose the pronunciation of Lu area and of the Chou period, and use the characters as used in the classics."[90]

The uncritical devotion to and the foolish imitation of the Chinese culture, TOMINAGA said, was meaningless and was contrary to the truth of the Confucian teaching. "Confucianists say, 'Do as the aliens do if you are in the alien community.' Also is it said, 'The Rite follows the local customs.' Then it is not that the Confucian scholars demand everybody to imitate the Chinese manners and customs. It is against the truth of Confucian teaching that the Confucianists of Japan would blindly practice what are alien to the Japanese, in the desire to imitate everything Chinese."[91]

TOMINAGA Nakamoto rejected the position of the contemporary Shinto also. Although his "Mahāyāna non-Buddhist" thesis was highly appreciated by the Shintoists because it provided a powerful means for the Shintoists to attack the Buddhists, TOMINAGA did not refrain from rebuking Shinto position for the lack of historical perspective. In spite of the continuity, Japan today and Japan in the Divine Antiquity had different manners and customs, and the thorough revivalism to antiquity would inevitably result in the most absurd confusion.

"In early Japan, the salutation of meeting was to crap hands toward the person and to bow four times; rice was eaten on a leaf of a tree; at mourning, people sang songs and wept aloud; when mourning was over, people went to a river and bathed in order to be released from pollution." Students of Shinto deliberately follow these customs, provided that they would conform to the ancient ways. As money did not exist in the Divine Antiquity, the students of Shinto should refrain from using money no matter how important it is today. They shall not wear the contemporary clothing as the style is a recent introduction during Wu times. They shall learn the ancient language and naming. For example, they shall address their father *kazo,* their mother *iroha,* etc."[92]

The vice of Shinto was that it neglected the historicity. "The practice of Shinto today is not the truth of Shinto. It advertizes curious and meaningless behavior while taking its model in the ancient customs."[93]

Ethics ought to be relevant to the particular chronological and spatial condition in which the specific person was located. "We must realize that it is very difficult and absurd to attempt to imitate the customs of China and India or to try to revive the practice of the Divine Antiquity, when the customs differ within the distance of ten or twenty miles and when the event of five or ten years ago is hardly remembered. The imitation, if it should happen to be perfect, is meaningless because the background differs. These three religions, therefore, are not the ways to be practiced in Japan today."[94]

TOMINAGA emphasized the contemporaneity of the meaning of history. "To write with the present-day script, to use present-day vernacular, to eat present-day food, to dress in present-day clothes, to use present-day utensils, to live in present-day houses, to follow present-day regulations, to mix with present-day people, to do nothing bad, to do all good things —that is the Way of Truth. That is the Way which is practicable in present-day Japan."[95]

It is not that TOMINAGA rejected the truth involved in the three religions, but that he opposed the attitude of the people that were blindly involved in one of the three teachings and that could not reflect on the

historical and endemic situation of the human being. He did not agree
with the people who attempted to apply the ethical principles of other
countries or of different ages to the present-day Japan. "I am not demanding the abolishment of the three religions. What I mean is to emphasize
the truth in them."[96] That is, TOMINAGA wanted to eliminate such situation that "the ways practiced today are superficial plays around Shinto,
Confucianism or Buddhism losing sight of the truth in Shinto, Confucianism or Buddhism."[97] Neither was he a popular syncretist of the three
religions. He intentionally rejected the thesis of some Chinese Buddhists
that all the religions were uniform, because he did not think that the
syncretists grasped the ultimate reason in the individual religions.

The most noteworthy feature of his thought is that he transported the
cause of morality from the Divine authority to the human existence.
Denying the traditional manner of authetication, he said, "The Way of
Truth is not come from either India or China. Nor is it an invention of
the Divine Antiquity which we have revived. It is not come from the
heaven or the earth either. It is the question of the present-day people.
It is the common sense in our daily life. If it is done, others are pleased
and the doer is pleasant, and everything goes well. If it is not done, others
are irritated and the idle is unpleasant, and everything goes ill. Therefore
it is done naturally from the experience of daily life. It is not an artificial
product with particular intention."[98]

In the west, the humanism of early modern period was born from the
realization of the human dignity and the struggle of its detachment from
the yoke of the traditional authorities. TOMINAGA's humanism was an
oriental counterpart of it. Only upon such humanist realization he could
initiate the philological studies of the classical literature.

Whether ethics may stand only upon the ground of humanism or not
is problematic, and yet his contention as such has the importance that
does not allow us to overlook it.

TOMINAGA pursued the study of the general history of philosophies,
or the general history of ethical thoughts with the consciousness such as
described above. There is no denying that Japan had competent philol-
ogues before and after him. All of them, however, were either Buddhist,

Confucianist or Shintoist, and were bound by the dogma of respective disciplines. TOMINAGA alone could clarify independence from any discipline. He declared, "I am not a disciple of Confucianism, nor of Shinto, nor of Buddhism. I am an observer of all the philosophies and discuss them from my own standard."[99] He was the first who wrote a systematic history of oriental philosophies with the new historic and endemic perspective. *Shutsujō Kōgo* (The Historical Survey of Buddhism) was so excellent a dissertation that the contemporary studies of the history of Buddhism go along the line that TOMINAGA opened so many years ago. His treatise on the history of Chinese philosophies *Seppei* (The Failings of the Classical Philosophers) is unfortunately lost, but its outline is surmised from another remaining work, *Okina no Fumi* (The Testament of an Old Man). TOMINAGA never thought any philosophy was absolute, and endeavored to clarify the meaning of each system in the historical and the endemic context.

We have sketched the Way of Truth of TOMINAGA Nakamoto. We would classify this "Way of the Ways" as "an ethical philosophy of ethical philosophies."

Particularism

Thus the ethical philosophy of TOMINAGA Nakamoto was the best characterized by the emphasis upon the historic and endemic particularity. The valuation of the particular, however, has been traditional in the way of thinking of the Japanese people in general. The earliest of such example, as far as we can trace, was the text criticism of the Japanese Buddhists during the Heian period (794–1192). The Tendai critics emphasized the importance of the matters (*ji*), while its Chinese counterpart the T'ien-t'ai scholars mainly worked on the principle (*ri*). The matters were the specific or particular being bound by the spatial and timely conditions. This trend was the most clearly revealed in the text criticism of Nichiren (1222–1282) who constructed his thesis on the ground of the Japanese Tendai doctrine. Nichiren proposed to classify the Buddhist teachings into five categories, which he called "the five religious dimensions," "the five levels of understanding," or "the five phases of Buddhism." The five categories were the content of the teaching in the scripture, the spiritual quality of the people whom the teaching was addressed, the need and the situation of the time at which the teaching was delivered, the particularity of the land where the teaching was preached, and the religious or philosophical conditions prior to the evangelization by the teaching. The proposition was that the teachings were to be evaluated and given order in reference to these five categories. Saichō (767–822), the founder of Japanese Tendai, had already discussed the importance of the elements of time and land, but he did not go to the extent of defining them the spinal code of the sect. Nichiren was the one who advanced the thesis to the maximum. And he was the first to introduce the category of the religious or philosophical conditions. The philosophical current of emphasizing the matters which found its ultimate expression in Nichiren was never developed either in India or in China. The Tendai and Nichiren way of criticizing other philosophies showed much in common with the way of criticism of TOMINAGA Nakamoto.

The same type of contention was recognized among the Confucianists of Japan. NAKAE Tōju (1608–1648), who held that the Confucian teaching was the absolute way applicable universally, considered that the way appeared differently in accordance with the difference of the time, the space and the social position in which each man was placed.

"As Confucianism is the eternal way of God, the way of CONFUCIUS is alive wherever there is a human being, wherever boats and carts reach, wherever heaven covers and earth holds, wherever the sun and the moon shine and wherever there is frost or mist. But the rites and the manners prescribed in the book of CONFUCIUS need not and cannot be practiced at different times, or at different places, or by different men."[100]

Tōju taught to "practice the rites and manners according to the way as accepted by the practice of the native community."[101] He believed that the Japanese observed the eternal way of God by following the way of Shinto. KUMAZAWA Banzan (1619–1691) thought similarly. According to him, there existed only one single way, the way of gods of heaven and earth. The way, however, appeared in different forms at different places. The monosanguineous lineage of the Emperors of Japan and the occasional revolutions of the dynasties of China must not be taken as the two different ways, but they should be regarded as the different expressions of the same way. "In Japan there are innate merits of merits of Japan alone."[102] KUMAZAWA then could revere Shinto as the way of Japan while remaining a Confucianist. "The way of God of heaven and earth is the Great Way, whose expression in Japanese land and water is Shinto." "Shinto at the Japanese land and water cannot be stored here or there, nor is it rentable somewhere."[103]

The way of thinking of these Confucian scholars came very close to that of the traditional Japanese Buddhist philosophers in the emphasis of the particurality over the universality of the truth. The only difference was that the Confucianists spoke of the endemic particularity whereas the Buddhists emphasized the historical particularity, eschatology being an example of the latter.

We are not sure if TOMINAGA was influenced by the thoughts of Tendai philosophers and Nichiren, or NAKAE Tōju and KUMAZAWA Banzan. But we are convinced that TOMINAGA and others developed their theses toward the same direction of recognizing the value in the particular.

The most exhaustive "philosophy of philosophies" ever constructed by the Japanese, we would presume, was the theory of consciousness by Kūkai (774–835). We must also pay attention to the philosophies of text criticism developed among the Tendai scholars. They were, however, the additions to or diviations from the text criticism of the Chinese Buddhism. They were, we should understand, the Japanese versions of the Chinese text criticism that came to being as the Chinese metamorphosis of the Indian way of thinking. Shintoists, on the other hand, did not formulate anything similar to a philosophy of philosophies by the medieval period, in spite of the efforts to fuse the continental philosophies into native way of thinking. In addition, the exclusive National Learning of Tokugawa Japan invited the sterility of such activities. Therefore we would commend the thought of TOMINAGA Nakamoto as the unique example of Japanese philosophy of philosophies.

The criticism of and the evaluation of all the world views from such a viewpoint as TOMINAGA had taken, i.e. that of historically specified "present-day Japan," had never been attempted either in India or in China. We recognize in this the typically Japanese outlook on the world.

Such outlook on the world or such philosophy of philosophies, in criticizing and evaluating all the philosophies from the viewpoint of the present-day Japan, would eventually arrive at ethno-centrism or state-centrism at the extreme of spatial specification, and to opportunism or conventionalism at the extreme of chronological specification. This means that this viewpoint includes the danger to neglect the universal law breaking through the chronological and spatial divisiveness. This viewpoint is at the opposite extreme of the Indian outlook of the world.[104]

It is said that the first "philosophy of philosophies" or "philosophy of histories of philosophies" was made known by the works of HEGEL. But it is true only so long as the history of philosophies in Europe originating from Greece is concerned. If we turn our attention to cultural areas other than Europe, e.g. India, we immediately recognize a good number of works achieved along the line. We must also recognize that the Indian way of dealing with this field of learning has been quite different from the modern European way. The modern Germanic and the medieval Indian views of the world must be distinguished. We must also distinguish the TOMINAGA view of the world from either of these. We would deem it necessary to classify it in the independent type, the Japanese view of the world.

HEGEL stated that there was no realization of the individuality but that there was all-embracing universalism in the Orient. The statement described well the characteristics of the Indian way of thinking. We would admit that the Indian have dealt with and evaluated the conflicting philosophies or outlooks of the world in terms of the universally applicable principle. The Japanese scholars as represented by TOMINAGA Nakamoto, however, showed a radically different approach to the question. We would not, therefore, agree with the statement of HEGEL above, if it meant to be applied to all the oriental philosophies.

1 *Religionssoziologische Schriften,* II, S. 296–297.
2 淨土眞宗.
3 Ibid., S. 304–305.
4 Ibid., S. 303.
5 気分, Ibid., S. 304.
6 *Kuden Hōmon*: 口伝法門, "Esoteric Teaching by Oral Tradition."
7 宗要抄.
8 OGATA Michinori, "Chūko Tendai no Keizai Rinri Kannen" 中古天台の経済倫理観念 (The Concept of Economical Ethics in Medieval Tendai). *Indogaku Bukkyōgaku Kenkyū* 印度学仏教学研究 (Study on Hindu and Buddhist Thought), 1958, March, VI, No. 2, pp. 110–111. See also the same author's "Kuden Hōmon no Jissen Rinri" 口伝法門の実践倫理 (Practical Ethics of Kuden Hōmon), *Nihon Bukkyō* 日本仏教 (Japanese Religion), 1958, October, No. 2, p. 44.
9 鈴木正三.
10 武士.
11 三河国東加茂郡則定郷 (盛岡村), 松平.
12 九太夫.
13 関ヶ原の役.
14 元和六年.
15 得度, (Entrance into the Buddhist priesthood), 大愚和尚, 臨済宗.
16 寛永, 石平山恩真寺.
17 慶安.
18 明暦.
19 曹洞宗, 道元.
20 普化.
21 玄俊.
22 破吉利支丹.
23 邪法.
24 万民徳用.
25 士農工商.
26 The Japanese translation of Robert N. BELLAH, *Tokugawa Religion, Nihon Kindaika to Shūkyō Rinri* 日本近代化と宗教倫理 (Japanese Modernization and Religious Ethics), translated by HORI Ichirō 堀一郎, and IKEDA Hidetoshi 池田英俊, Miraisha, 1962, p. 179, p. 191, p. 207.

27 二宮尊徳.

28 蓮如.

29 座禅 umbilicular contemplation.

30 SUZUKI Shōsan, *Roankyō* 驢鞍橋, 1660, II, 89.

31 Ibid., III, p. 19.

32 All the quotations are taken from Shōsan's works or his memoirs which are compiled in *Zemmon Hōgoshū* 禅門法語集 edited by YAMADA Kōdō 山田孝道 and MORI Daikyō 森大狂, *Kokubun Tōhō Bukkyō Soshō* 国文東方仏教叢書 by WASHIO Junkei 鷲尾順敬 and *Suzuki Shōsan Dōjin Zenshū* 鈴木正三道人全集 by SUZUKI Tesshin (Sankibō Busshorin, 1962 and others).

This paper is written on the basis of the author's *Kinsei Nihon ni okeru Hihanteki Seishin no Ichikōsatsu* 近世日本に於ける批判的精神の一考察 (A Study of the Critical Spirit in Modern Japan) Sanseidō, 1949 (also in *Gendai Bukkyō Meicho Zenshū* 現代仏教名著全集, Ryūbunkan 隆文館, Tokyo, 1960. II).

33 *Tamakatsuma*, vol. 8

34 *Shutsujō Shōgo,* vol. 3, (*Social History of Buddhism*)

35 See 中村元, "Critical Spirit of Pre-modern Japan" 1965:『出定後語註解』pp. 255-303,『翁の文註解』pp. 305-307.

36 E.g.「集解標旨鈔」

37 E.g.「法苑珠林」,「大乗義章」,「法苑義林章」
「天台三大部」,「華厳五教章」,「翻訳名義集」
He may have read part of *Tripitaka*. Some of his quotations correspond to the *Tripitaka* of Ming edition, while different from other editions. In reference to the legend that TOMINAGA stayed at Obakusan which published the *Tripitaka* of Ming edition, it could have been possible that he had occasions to read it. But this surmise is not strong enough to repudiate our thesis that he did not read it much.

38 *Shutsjō Shōgo* vol. 3.

39 *Shutsjō Kōgo* vol. 24 (Historical Survey of Buddhism)

40 Ibid., vol. 22.

41 *Daichidoron* 大智度論 (Mahāprajñāpāramitopadeśa), vol. 18 in *Taishō Tripitaka*. vol. 25, p. 192. *Mo-ho-chih-kuan* 摩訶止観 (Various Aspects of Meditation), vol. 6a in *Taishō Tripitaka* vol. 46, p. 73.

42 *T'ien-t'ai-ssū-chiao-i*, 天台四教義 (Four Fundamental Doctrines in the Tíen-tái Sect) in *Taishō Tripitaka,* vol. 46, p. 724

43 *Uiyamabumi* うひやまぶみ (Essays of Motoori Norinaga)

44 *Bemmei*「弁名」vol. 1. 善良三則 (Discourse on Name).

45 「翁の文」*Okina no Fumi* (Testament of an Old Man).

46 「顕揚正法復古集」vol. 1. in 村上専精「大乗仏説論批判」pp. 84
「香海一滴」in 前田恵雲「大乗仏教史論」p.p. 278-280

47 敬首律師「真如祕稿」

48 村上 p. 116 ff. 前田 pp. 281-283.

49 He was not an observer of the commandments. He did not think drinking was prohibited. See *Shutsujō Kōgo*, ch. 14-16.

50 Ibid. 8

51 Ibid.

52 Ibid.

53 Based on the *Analects of Confucius*.

54 *Okina no Fumi*, ch. 15 (Translation in Theodore DE BURY ed. *Sources of Japanese Tradition* (1958) p. 487–488).

55 *Shutsujō Kōgo*, ch. 8

56 *Okina no Fumi*, ch. 14

57 *Shutsujō Kōgo*, ch. 8

58 Ibid., ch. 8
  Ibid., ch. 25,「異却幻変の説」
  Ibid., ch. 25,「無量劫を以てする者は幻の幻なり」

59 Ibid., ch. 8

60 *Okina no Fumi*, comm.「神通は修行より出る」

61 *Shutsujō Kōgo*, ch. 25

62 Ibid., ch. 24

63 Ibid., ch. 15, 25

64 Ibid., ch. 24

65 Ibid.

66 Ibid.

67 Ibid., ch. 8

68 *Okina no Fumi* ch. 16   (DE BURY, p. 488).

69 Ibid., ch. 16   (DE BURY, p. 488).

70 Ibid., ch. 9

71 *Shutsujō Kōgo*, ch. 9

72 Ibid., ch. 6

73 H. A. KORFF. *Humanismus und Romantik* (1924), S. 10.

74 Quotations below otherwise specified are from Chapters 11 and 25 of the *Historical Survey of Buddhism*.

75 Mencius.「親之過小而怨，是不可磯也」
Chao Chih.「磯激也」
Chu Hsi.「磯水激石也，不可磯言微激之而遽怒也」

76 *Gakuritsu-kō*「楽律考」[*Discourse on Music*].

77 *Okina no Fumi*, preface (DE BURY. Op. cit., p. 483).

78 Ibid., p. 484–485.

79 Ibid., p. 485.

80 *Shutsujō Kōgo*, ch. 25, the miscellany.

81 Ibid., ch. 14 (Precept).

82 Ibid., ch. 24 (Three teachings).

83 *Okina no Fumi*, ch 6 annotation (DE BURY, p. 485).

84 Ibid., ch. 6 (DE BURY, p. 484).

85 Ibid., ch. 5

86 Ibid., ch. 1 (DE BURY, pp. 483–484).

87 Ibid., ch. 2, 3

88 Ibid., ch. 1

89 *Gobunritsu* 五分律 vols. 2–3 in *Taishō Tripitaka*, vol. 22, p. 153

90, 91 *Okina no Fumi*, ch. 2

92, 93, 94, 95 Ibid., ch. 5

96, 97 Ibid., ch. 8

98 Ibid., ch. 7

99 *Shutsujō Kōgo*, ch. 24., three teachings.

100 *Okina Mondō* 翁問答, vol. 3. *Tōju Sensei Zenshū* (Complete Work of NAKAE Tōju), vol. 3., pp. 248–249.

101 Ibid., the 94th. dialogue, p. 251).

102 *Miwa Monogatari* 三輪物語 *Banzan Zenshū* (Complete Work of KUMAZAWA Banzan), vol. 248, p. 249
(See FISHER, GALEN. "Kumazawa Banzan. His Life and Ideals." *Translations of the Asiatic Society of Japan*, 2nd ser., XVI (1938), pp. 221–58).

103 HIYANE Antei, *Nihon Shūkyō-Shi* 日本宗教史 (History of Japanese Religions) (1938), pp. 221–58

104 NAKAMURA Hajime, *Tetsugaku-teki Shisaku no Indo-teki Tenkai* [哲学的思索の印度的展開] (1949), pp. 1–68.

CHAPTER VII

PROBLEMS OF JAPANESE PHILOSOPHICAL THOUGHT

1. Basic Features of the Legal, Political and Economic Thought

The legal, political, and economical thought of a people cannot be discussed without taking the chief basic philosophical concepts of the people into consideration. Professor Northrop says: "In fact, the philosophy of any society is but the name for the basic concepts and assumptions agreed upon by its people for organizing the data of their experience and ordering their relation to nature and to one another."[1] Among the main features of Japanese ways of thinking we must note the following three:

(1) *Acceptance of actuality.* (1) Apprehension of the absolute in the phenomenal world; (2) "this-worldliness"; (3) acceptance of natural human qualities; (4) the spirit of tolerance; (5) cultural stratification; and (6) weakness of the spirit of direct criticism.

(11) *Tendency to emphasize a particular social nexus.* (1) Emphasis on human relations; (2) human relationships of greater importance than the individual; (3) absolute view of limited social organization; (4) reverence for family morality; (5) emphasis upon hierarchical relations of status; (6) the supremacy of the state; (7) absolute obedience to a particular person; (8) emperor worship; (9) closed character of sects and cliques; (10) protection of the particular social nexus by force; (11) emphasis on activity in society; (12) sensitivity to moral introspection; and (13) lack of self-consciousness in religious reverence.

(111) *Non-rational tendencies.* (1) Non-logical tendencies; (2) weakness in ability to think in terms of logical consequences; (3) intuitional and

emotional tendencies; (4) lack of ability to form complex representations; (5) fondness for simple, symbolical representations; (6) weakness in knowledge of objective processes.[2]

Esteem for Human Nature

In general, the Japanese are inclined to search for the absolute within the phenomenal world or in what is actual. Among all the natures that are given and real, the most immediate to man is the nature of man. Hence the Japanese tend to esteem highly man's natural disposition. So, as one of the most prominent features of traditional Japanese ways of thinking, we may point out the emphasis on the love of human beings. This might be described as the naturalistic view of life.[3] This tendency has been conspicuous among Shintoists. Buddhist idea have also been taught with close reference to matters of love, and even sexual love is considered to be not incompatible with religious matters. The tendency to esteem man's nature gave rise to the love of human beings in reality.

The tendency toward humanitarianism has been traditional among the Japanese; yet it has generally escaped the attention of scholars. The love of others in its purest form is called "benevolence" (Sanskrit: *maitri, karuna*). This idea was introduced into Japan with the advent of Buddhism. The attempt to realize universal religions in politics caused rulers to deal with people affectionately and compassionately, as in the case of Asoka, who said: "All people are my children."

Prince Shōtoku (574–622) asserted: "As the disease of infatuation among the common people is endless, the compassionate measures taken up by bodhisattvas also are endless. . . . Common people are of less beatitude; we teach them to do meritorious deeds. . . . Properties are what can save people from poverty and affliction. So Buddhas save living beings in various areas with the Four All-Embracing Virtues, the Four Virtues of Infinite Greatness, and the Six Perfections." Prince Shōtoku emphasized "harmony" or "concord" in human relations. With deep self-reflection, he advocated such concord in the first article of his Constitution: "Above all else esteem concord; make it your first duty to avoid discord. People are prone to form partisanship, for few persons are really enlightened. Hence there are those who do not obey lords and parents, and they come in conflict with their neighbors. But when those above are harmonious and those below are friendly, there is concord in the discussion of affairs, and right views of things spontaneously gain acceptance. Then what could not be accomplished?"

Some scholars say that the conception of concord (*wa*) here was adopted from Confucianism, for the word *wa* is used in *The Analects of Confucius*. But the term "*wa*" was used in connection with propriety or decorum in that work,[4] and concord was not the subject there. Prince Shōtoku, on the other hand, advocated concord as the principle of human behavior.[5] His attitude seems to have derived from the Buddhist concept of benevolence, which should be distinguished from the Confucian.

The Constitution of Prince Shōtoku esteems the welfare of the people and is sympathetic toward them. The fifth article teaches sympathy with suffering people in law suits. Other articles also contain such admonitions as: "Such are the kinds of men who are never loyal to the lord, nor benevolent toward the people. All this is the source from which grave civil disturbances occur" (Article VI). "Provincial governors and district administrators should not levy exacting taxes on their respective peoples" (Article XII). In the Constitution common people came to have some significant role in the consciousness of the ruling class. This role could not be destroyed in later history, and the trend might be regarded as the first step in the gradual development of democracy.

King Asoka also endeavored greatly to promote cultivation of medical herbs. "Wherever medical herbs, wholesome for men and wholesome for animals, are not found, they have everywhere been caused to be imported and planted. Roots and fruits, wherever they are not found, have been caused to be imported and planted." Prince Shōtoku also, together with his officials, carried on a "hunt for medical herbs," and established dispensaries.

The spirit of benevolence was preached not only by the Buddhists; it also made its way into Shintoism, and was tied up with one of the three divine symbols of the Japanese Imperial Family, which claimed to rule on the spiritual basis of benevolence. The Tokugawa Shogunate inherited this attitude. Benevolence also came to be regarded as one of the principal virtues of the *samurai*, who asserted that it was not sufficient for them to be physically brave and strong, but that they should be compassionate with the common people.[6] Japanese Confucian scholars of politics also lay special emphasis upon the love of others. KUMAZAWA Banzan, a famous Confucianist of the Tokugawa period, called Japan "the land of benevolence."[7] These facts give ample testimony to the assumption that the ruling class of Japan aimed at benevolence as their principal ideal.

In pre-Buddhist Japan, cruel punishments were not lacking; emperors killed their subjects arbitrarily.[8] On the occasions of the interment of emperors, their retainers were buried alive around their graves.[9] Such customs were eventually abolished, and after the advent of Buddhism there existed in Japan hardly any punishment that could be called cruel. During the Heian period, capital punishment was not practiced for about three hundred and fifty years. Since crucifixion appeared for the first time in Japanese history during the Age of the Civil Wars, it was probably introduced after the advent of Christianity and suggested by it.

The love of human beings seems to be closely connected with the love of the beauties of Nature, which is as old as the Japanese people themselves. CHIANG Monlin describes the Asian way of knowing nature as follows: "The Chinese people are devoted to nature, not in the sense of finding the natural laws but in the sense of cultivating the poetic, artistic, or moral sense as lovers of nature." This holds true for the Japanese attitude also.

The features pointed out here give us some clues to the basic concepts of Japanese legal, political, and economic thought.

The Spirit of Harmony or Concord

The unanimous moral solidarity of a community has been aimed at as the social ideal, on an island scale, in Japan. This was felt intuitively in the spiritual atmosphere of the primitive society of Japan. Later, when the centralized state was established after the conflicts among various tribes had ended, what was stressed in the first place as the principle of the community was "concord." According to the Sixteen Article Law (as set forth in the *Chronicle of Tibet*); "Whosoever quarrels, is punished severely" (Article 1). Asoka also stressed the spirit of concord (*samavāya*). In the same way, men are apt to be bigoted and partial. Inside a community or between communities, conflicts are sure to occur. One should overcome such conflicts, and concord should be realized, so that a harmonious community may be formed in an ideal way. The spirit of concord was stressed throughout all the articles of the Constitution. Concord between lord and subject, between superior and inferior, among people in general and among individuals, was taught repeatedly. This concord is essentially nothing but concord, not obedience.

Prince Shōtoku did not teach that the people should merely follow or obey, but that discussion should be carried on in an atmosphere of concord or harmony, so that one might attain right views. Earnest discussion was most desirable.

King Asoka said: "Let us cease from wrath, and refrain from angry looks. Nor let us be resentful just because others oppose us. Every person has a mind of his own; each heart has its own learning. We may regard as wrong what they hold as right. We are not unquestionably sages, nor are they assuredly fools. Both of us are simply ordinary men. Who is wise enough to judge which of us is good or bad? For we are all wise and foolish alternately, like a ring which has no end. Therefore, although others may give way to anger, let us on the contrary dread our own faults, and though we may be sure that we are in the right, let us act in harmony with many others." (Article X)[10]

If we discuss affairs with this feeling of harmony—desisting from anger —difficult problems will be settled spontaneously and in the right way. In this way alone is it possible that decisions can be reached at conferences.

King Asoka also asserts the necessity for self-reflection: "(A person) seeth the good deed only (saying unto himself:) 'This good deed has been done by me.' In no wise doth he see (his) sin (saying unto himself:) 'this sin have I committed,' or 'this, indeed, is a depravity.' But this certainly is difficult to scrutinize. Nevertheless, it should certainly be looked into thus: 'these (passions), indeed, lead to depravity, such as violence, cruelty, anger, conceit, envy and by reason thereof may I not cause my fall.' "

The democratic way of managing a conference was realized in the remote past. In the mythology which reflects the primitive society of Japan, deities convened in divine assembly in the bed of a river. This tradition was followed and developed by later monarchs.

Setting forth multifarious mental attitudes of rulers and officials, Prince Shōtoku, in Article XVII, denounced dictatorship and stressed the necessity of discussing things with others: "Decisions on important matters should generally not be made by one person alone. They should be discussed with many others. But small matters are of less importance, and it is unnecessary to consult many persons concerning them. In the case of discussing weighty matters you must be fearful lest there be faults. You should arrange matters in consultation with many persons, so as to arrive at the right conclusion."

This represents the beginning of Japanese democratic thought, for Article XVII corresponds to the first Article, to the effect that discussion should be carried on in the spirit of concord.

This trend developed into an edict after the Taika Innovation (645), which thus denounced the dictatorship of a sovereign: "Things should not be instituted by a single ruler."

Whence has the denunciation of dictatorship been inherited?

The ancient way of ruling represented in Japanese mythology is not dictatorship by a monarch or by the Lord of All, but a conference of gods in a river bed. Where public opinion was not esteemed, a conference could not have been held successfully: hence the spirit of primitive Shintoism must have been inherited and developed by later rulers.

On the other hand, it is possible that the rules of the Buddhist order influenced the thought of the Prince, rules set forth in full detail in the scriptures, including the rules of decision by majority. The fact that consultation with many others was not explicitly encouraged by Asoka, nor by Songtsan-Gampo, but by Prince Shōtoku, is noteworthy. This ideal was preserved in the days when the emperors were in power: Japanese monarchy or the Emperor Institution developed as something different from dictatorship.

Professor NORTHROP observes that when a dispute arises among Asians, one does not settle it by recourse to determinate legal principles, but pursues the "middle way" of mediation between the determinate theses of the disputants, by fostering the all-embracing intuitively felt formlessness common to all men and things.[11]

This emphasis upon mediation rather than legal codes and litigation is the way to settle disputes in pre-Western Confucian China, Buddhist countries, and India. Prof. NORTHROP explains: "This does not mean that Buddhist of India, Thailand and Confucian Chinado not have codes. They do. But the attitude toward them is entirely different from that of the West. The proper way is not to use codes, but mediation. The code is regarded as an evil to be used as a last resort for settling disputes between immoral men when the moral way to the settling of disputes by intuitive feeling and mediation fails."[12]

CHIANG Monlin writes: "Modern legal sense as the West understands it is not developed in China. Avoid the courts if you can. Let us settle our disputes without going to law. Let's compromise. Let's have a cup of tea and sip together with friends and talk things over." This is exactly the situation we find among the countrymen of Japan also. There is a well-known Japanese proverb which is understood by everybody in practice: "In a quarrel both parties (the two) are to blame." This is not due to lack of esteem for law on the part of Japanese people, but to financial and other reasons. If people should go to court, they will lose much time; it may take them several years to settle even one case. They have to employ lawyers and spend much money. Even if they should win at court, they will eventually obtain very little. Hence resort to legal measures very often impairs (taking everything into account) the happiness and welfare of the people concerned and others around them. Barristers-at-law are not always respected, but very often abhorred, by the common people of Japan, from fear that they may take advantage of the people's lack of legal knowledge in order to make money. The writer personally knows some Japanese intellectuals who claim to be businessmen at home, but to be lawyers when they go abroad: They want to conceal their status as lawyers while they work among the Japanese.

But this does not mean that Japanese laws are applied partially. The Japanese give the same meanings for the expression of definite laws or codes, for all men and occasion; there is no difference at all. Yet they do not always want to resort to legal measures.

As the objective causes which brought about such a tendency in the Japanese people, we may cite the social life peculiar to their land and climate. The primitive Indo-Europeans, being nomadic and living chiefly by hunting, were in contact with alien peoples. Here, human relations were marked by fierce rivalry. Peoples were in great migration; one race conquered another, only to be conquered by still another. In such a society, struggles for existence were based not on mutual trust but on rational plan and strategem.

Japanese society, on the other hand, developed from small localized farming communities. The Japanese did away with nomadic life early, and settled down to cultivate rice fields. People living on rice must inevitably settle permanently in one place. In such a society *families* continue, generation after generation. Genealogies and kinships of families through long years become so well known by their members that the society as a whole takes on the appearance of a family. In such a society individuals are closely bound to each other and they form an exclusive human nexus. Here an individual who asserts himself will hurt the feelings of others and thereby do harm to himself. The Japanese learned to adjust themselves to this type of familial society, and created forms of expression suitable to life in it. Here grew the worship of tutelary gods and local deities. Even today there is a strong tendency in the Japanese social structure to settle closely around such tutelary gods and local deities. This tendency is deeply rooted in the people and has led to their stressing of human relations, especially the spirit of harmony or concord. The Japanese have learned to attach unduly heavy importance to the human nexus in disregard of the individual.

The Concept of Law

Professor NORTHROP says: "There is never a legal, political or economic society except when all the facts of that society are ordered by certain common normative or, in other words, ideological principles. Law and its political institutions, and one may add also economics and its business institutions, are effective only as they correspond to express this ideological or normative inner order."[13]

It seems that his opinion holds true for the Japanese also, when we consider that the Japanese people were brought to the form of a nation only at a time when laws, or at least normative forms, were established among the people.

Law-giving was not lacking even in the genuinely Shintoistic, pre-Buddhistic age. To illustrate, it is said that Emperor Seimu determined the frontiers and civilized the country, and that he issued laws. He reformed surnames and selected given names.[14] The laws of the primitive Japanese, as of all ancient peoples, were those of customs. Though their details have been lost, it is likely that the two fundamental principles—Imperial sovereignty and the family system—were firmly established even in those days. No positive law, however, is known to us from those days. It is with Prince Shōtoku that we first come to know something of laws in the modern sense.

Prince Shōtoku, the real founder of the centralized state of Japan, proclaimed the Seventeen-Article Constitution in 604. This was the first legislation in Japan, a characteristic expression of the original and creative development of the Japanese in those days—adopting the civilizations and thought of China and India, chiefly based upon the spirit of Buddhism. This is, so to speak, the Magna Charta of Japan. The Constitution prescribed the rules of conduct which the officials of the Imperial government should obey, thereby perchance revealing how badly needed such rules were. The Constitution was proclaimed about forty years prior to the Taika Innovation (Reform of 645).

It has been confirmed by scholars that there is a close connection between the spirit of Shōtoku's Constitution and the political regime established by the Taika Innovation, which accomplished the unified state of Japan.

In connection with Prince Shōtoku's Seventeen-Article Constitution: King Songtsan-Gampo, the founder of the centralized state of Tibet, proclaimed a Sixteen-Article Law of similar purport at nearly the same time; while, going back to antiquity, we find that King Asoka published many Rock and Pillar Edicts which proclaimed various precepts whose number was not fixed. The characteristic common to all of these documents is that they are approximate to moral precepts in the form of representation, and that they were different from positive laws in practice. The Tibetans were especially conscious of this point. According to them, the Sixteen-Article Law was Men's Law (mi-chos) which was different from Gods' Law (tha-chos). The former was an ethical law, whereas the latter was a religious one; both constitute the System of Laws (chos-lugs). King Asoka classified them both under the name of "Law" (dharma).

Based upon such fundamental laws, practical laws were instituted. The Tibetans called them "Laws of Ruling" (rgval-khrims). Songtsan-Gampo is said to have instituted laws to punish murder, theft and adultery. These correspond to the laws and rules since the Taika Innovation. The laws which were in practice in the Maruyan age around Asoka seem to have been incorporated into the Arthasāstra of Kautlya. Due to later interpolations in the work, however, it is very difficult to identify those which were composed in the Maruyan age. Nevertheless, there is one difference: Songtsan-Gampo's Law taught popular morals meant for common people, whereas Shōtoku's Constitution proclaimed the "Ways of the Public," i.e., mental and moral attitudes of officials concerning state affairs. The edicts of Asoka were mostly meant for common people; some, for officials. This difference betrays the fact that bureaucracy was very strong even at the outset of the centralized state of Japan, and it foretells the supremacy of bureaucrats in later-day Japan.

Positive laws were officially promulgated later. In 671, a code of laws, said to have consisted of twenty-two volumes, was collated; but the entire code was lost, and its contents are unknown. In 701, the work of codification was completed. This entire code, known as the Taiho Code, consisting of eleven volumes of general law concerning government organization, administration, and private relations, and six volumes of criminal law, was promulgated and enforced. Revised in 718, these Taiho laws, with many subsequent revisions and supplements, governed the nation for about five hundred years, until 1190.

With the establishment of a feudal regime, the individual Shoguns issued laws. As the authority of the Shoguns increased, the territory within which the Taiho laws were enforced decreased. In the Age of Civil Wars (1467–1585), many feudal lords issued their own regulations or family laws. The Tokugawa Shogunate (1603–1868) tried to govern the country according to already existing customs and, as far as possible, avoided the making of written laws. Contact with Western nations and a study of their civilization after the Meiji Restoration showed the necessity for laws in harmony with the modern world. In 1882, the criminal code was promulgated. This was followed in 1889 by the proclamation of a Constitution and, in 1900, by the civil code. Up to the end of World War II, Japanese law was characterized by the two fundamental principles mentioned earlier; the sovereignty of the Emperor, and the partriarchal family system. In 1946, after the surrender of Japan, a new constitution was promulgated, and the preceding principles were legally abolished, although they still exist in practice.

Professor NORTHROP says: "Only by mastering also this basically Western scientific and philosophical way of conceptualizing nature in terms of laws and concepts which are universals will they understand and apply effectively the Western type of political constitution, economic system and legal processes. For only through this form of knowledge is it possible for men to find the values transcending family loyalty necessary to make these Western social forms effective.[15]

The move to conceptualize human affairs in terms of laws and concepts which are universals has been effected by the Japanese to some extent. In the Rock and Pillar Edicts proclaimed to the subjects in general, freedom of thought is expressed, and no effort is made to teach that Buddhism alone should be esteemed. However, in an edict (the *Bhabru* inscription) issued to a Buddhist order, it is said that the monarch places faith in the Three Jewels, i.e., Buddha, the Law, and the Order. "King Priyadarsin of Magadha, having saluted the Sangha, wishes them good health and comfortable (bodily) movement. Ye know, Reverend Sirs, how great are my respect and kindliness towards Buddha, Dharma, and Sangha."

"The ordering of a theoretically directed world by means of legally drawn contracts, constitutions or charters is alien to the Asian of the villages,"[16] says Professor NORTHROP. He adds: "Truly the Greco-Roman Christian concept of moral, spiritual and legal man as an instance of universal law protects as well as presupposes liberty. This idea came to expression in the Middle Ages as much as in modern times. What is the Magna Charta but the thesis that even the King is subject, just like anyone else, to the law? His title to kingship is valid only if he accepts the divine logos as superior to himself."[17]

Then why had the Japanese in those days to resort to Buddhism?

The concept of universal law came into existence very early in the time of Prince Shōtoku, when he said: "Sincerely revere the Three Treasures. The Three Treasures, viz. the Buddha, the Law, and the Congregation, constitute the final ideal of all living beings and the ultimate foundation of all countries. Should any age or any people fail to esteem this truth? There are few men who are really vicious. They will all follow it if adequately instructed. How can the crooked ways of men be made straight, unless we take refuge in the Three Treasures?"[18] Here we find the concept of a universal law which is something beyond laws based on the inductive status of the individual in the joint family and of the family in its respective tribe or caste. According to the Prince, the "Law" is the "norm" of all living creatures; the "Buddhas" is in fact "the Law embodied," which, "being united with reason," becomes the *sangha*. So, according to his teaching, everything converges in the one fundamental principle called the "Law."

The Empress Suiko issued an Imperial edict to promote the prosperity of the Three Treasures in the year 594. It is said that, at that time, all the Ministers vied with one another in erecting Buddhist temples for the beatitude of their lords and parents. Thus the Buddhist culture came to take root, grew and blossomed. A new epoch in the cultural history of Japan began.

It is likely that other Asian kings who adopted Buddhism thought in the same way. Asoka, however, resorted to *dharma,* which is valid for various religions, and not necessarily Buddhism alone. Buddhism was nothing but one of many religions which received protection from him, just like Brahmanism, Jainism and the Ājīvikas, although it is certain that Asoka particularly patronized and supported Buddhism.

Things being so, it may seem that there was a fundamental difference between Asoka and other Asiatic monarchs, including Prince Shōtoku. Investigating the fundamental ideas which transformed these historical facts into reality, however, we find there was not much difference. In the case of Prince Shōtoku, there was only one philosophical system which taught universal laws—Buddhism. It was natural that the Prince should term Buddhism "the final ideal of all living beings and the ultimate foundation of all countries." In the case of Asoka, however, many religious systems had already become highly developed, and there were many other religions which claimed to be universal philosophical systems, so he had to take up many religions. When we examine matters more deeply, we find that according to the Prince the quintessence of Buddhism consists in acknowledging the universal laws taught by all religions and philosophies, as is evidenced in early and Mahāyāna Buddhism. Therefore we are led to the conclusion that there is no fundamental legalistic difference in outlook between King Asoka and Prince Shōtoku. In this respect they had this in common: that they wanted to found their kingdoms on the basis of universal laws or the truth of the universe.

Due to this characteristic of Buddhism, neither Prince Shōtoku nor King Songtsan-Gampo, not to mention Asoka, suppressed the indigenous faiths of their respective peoples, although they both esteemed and revered Buddhism. That is why Shintoism in Japan and the Bon religion in Tibet have been preserved up to the present. In Burma, the faith of Nats is prevalent even now among common people. Taking into consideration such an attitude we shall be able to understand why the following edict was proclaimed in the reign of Prince Shōtoku: "In my reign, why shall we be negligent of practicing the worship of Shintoist gods? All my officials should worship them sincerely." Both Shintoism and Buddhism have been given protection by the government throughout history. When we compare these facts with the situation in the West, we find a fundamental difference.

Christianity gradually came to the fore in spite of various persecutions. Freedom of faith was finally assured by Emperor Constantine with the edict of Milan in the year 313. Christianity became the state religion on the occasion of the unification of the state by Emperor Theodosius. The Eastern Roman Emperor Justinian, in 529, forbade the worship of heathen gods except the Christian God. These measures characterized the later theological development of Western culture.

Prince Shōtoku, on the other hand, established a new official organization, reforming the old regime under which the higher court ranks were hereditary. Under the new regime anyone could attain promotion according to his ability and merit without distinction of birth. This new system of appointment was called the Twelve Court Ranks (603). The same measures seem to have been taken up by the Maruyan dynasty, on the advice of Kautilya. As it was the officials who acted as the central figures in the newly established centralized states, their moral had to be firmly maintained.

Some Western intellectuals say that Eastern peoples make no distinction between good and bad, right and wrong. But Prince Shōtoku taught that the spirit of esteeming good and hating bad should be cherished: "Punish the vicious and reward the virtuous. This is the excellent rule of antiquity. Do not, therefore, let the good deeds of any person go concealed, nor the bad deeds of any go uncorrected, when you see them. Flatterers and deceivers are like the fatal missile which will overthrow the state, or the sharp sword which will destroy the people. Likewise sycophants are fond of telling their superiors the errors of their inferiors; to their inferiors, they censure the faults of the superiors. Such are the kind of men who are never loyal to the lord, nor benevolent toward the people. All this is the source from which grave civil disturbances occur."

(Article VI) This spirit can be traced in the case of King Asoka of old, who deplored that good deeds are difficult to effect, whereas bad ones are easy to do: "Good is difficult to perform. He who initiates good does something difficult to perform. Hence by me much good had been done. If my sons, grandsons, and my descendants after them, until the aeon of destruction, follow similarly, they will do what is meritorious, but in this respect he who abandons even a part (here), will do ill. Verily, sin is easy to commit."[19] In the scripture of early Buddhism it is also taught: "Evil deeds, deeds which are harmful to oneself, are easy to do. What is beneficial and good, that is very difficult to do."[20] Moreover, the Prince wrote: "Light crimes should be embraced by our power of reforming influence, and grave crimes should be surrendered to our power of strong force."[21] He did not avoid resorting to force in order to punish the severely wicked.

In *"Bushidō,"* or "the Way of Knights," which developed in later times as the peculiarly Japanese "way," and which was regarded as the actual political philosophy of the Japanese, the distinction between good and bad was extremely stressed and strictly observed. *"Bushi"* or Knights should do nothing mean or despicable even at the cost of their lives.

Considering these historical facts, the assertion made by some scholars that Westerners are keen in the rigid distinction between good and bad, whereas the Eastern peoples are not, is untenable.

"In hearing judicial cases of common people judges should banish avaricious desires and give up their own interest. Deal impartially with the suits brought by the people. Of the cases to be tried, there are a thousand each day. If so many in one day, there will be immense numbers of disputes to be settled in a series of years. Nowadays it is alleged that some judges seek their own profit, and attend to the cases after having taken bribes, which as given rise to the saying: 'The suits of the rich men are like the stone cast into the pond, whereas the suits of the poor men are like water thrown upon a rock.' Hence the poor people do not know where to betake themselves. Such a state of affairs, if brought about, would mean a deficiency in the duty of officials." (Article V)

King Asoka also taught the officials that they should aim at the happi-

ness and welfare of people, and that for that purpose they should observe the utterances, ordinances, and instructions of *dharma*. He esteemed forbearance and lightness of punishment.[22] "Each person has a
duty to perform; let not the spheres of duty be confused. When wise and
capable persons are entrusted with high offices, there will arise a unanimous voice of pleased approval; but when wicked persons hold high
offices, disasters and disturbances are multiplied. In this world there are
few who are endowed with inborn wisdom; sainthood is the goal attained after long self-discipline. All matters of State, whether great or
small, will surely be well ordered, when right persons are in the right
position in any periods, whether critical or peaceful, all affairs will be
peacefully settled, when wise men are secured. In this way will the State
be lasting, and the realm be free from dangers. Therefore the wise
sovereigns of ancient times sought good men for high offices, and not
good offices for favored ones." (Article VII) "All officials, high and low,
should beware of jealousy. If you are jealous of others, others in turn
will be jealous of you and so is perpetuated the vicious circle. So if we
find others excel us in intelligence, we are not pleased; if we find they
surpass us in ability, we become envious. Really wise persons are seldom
seen in this world—possibly one wise man in five centuries or one sage
in ten centuries. Without securing wise men and sages, wherewith shall
the country be governed in good order?" (Article XIV)

Nationalism and Imperial Prestige

It has been often pointed out that the basic social and moral principles
of Asian peoples consist essentially of filial piety. Professor NORTHROP
says: "The basic social and moral principle of this joint family is filial
piety—where by filial piety is meant not merely loyalty to one's father
and mother, but loyalty to this joint family. Hinduism and Buddhism
may not feature the concept of filial piety as do Confucian Asian families,
but the fact is nonetheless there."[23]

With regard to the Japanese, this feature holds true to some extent, but
not wholly. In Japan, loyalty to lords in the days since the Meiji Restoration have been much stronger.

The peculiarly Japanese conception of the prestige of the emperor and the Emperor Institution bear a close relation to the traditionally fundamental conception of harmony. The atmosphere of "harmony" which has prevailed between the emperor and his subjects has enabled the Emperor Institution to last as long as the institution which has been characteristic of the political history of Japan. In other countries dynasties changed. But in Japan there has been only one ruling dynasty or royal family; it has no specific family name, thus evidencing the remote antiquity of its rulership. This dynasty has never been broken during its long history of more than two thousand years. In the past, the emperor was looked at as a child of the Sun Deity, but not with awe. In olden days, the prestige of a deity was superior to that of an emperor. In the genuinely Shintoistic, pre-Buddhistic Japan, an emperor who was compassionate with the people was respected with affection as an ideal monarch (as illustrated in the person of Nintoku).

In the case of the Prince an intention which was hardly shown in the cases of monarchs of other countries is expressed, until in later days the prestige of the emperor came to be closely connected with the hierarchical order of Japanese society.

"When you receive the orders of the Sovereign, you should listen to them reverentially. The lord is like the heavens and the subjects are like the earth. With the heavens above and the earth below united in performing their functions loyally in their respective positions, we shall see the world ruled in perfect good order as in harmonious rotation of the four seasons. . . . If the earth should attempt to supplant the heavens, all would simply fall in ruin. Therefore when the lord speaks, let his subjects listen and obey; when the superiors act, the inferiors comply. Consequently when you receive the orders of the Sovereign you should be attentive in carrying them out faithfully. If you fail in this, ruin would be the natural consequence." (Article III)

The intention of having his edicts observed among the common people was very strong in the case of Asoka also. Having the edicts inscribed on the stone pillars erected by him, or on the polished surface of rocks, was aimed at their being read by the common people. Asoka said: "Since

I was consecrated twelve years, I have caused Edicts of *dharmas* to be written for the welfare and happiness of the people, so that without violation thereof, they might attain to this and that growth of *dharma*."

It is needless to note that those who could read and understand the edicts must have been limited only to the classes of rulers and intellectuals in those days. However, those who were impressed by the sentences of the edicts must have amounted to a considerable number. Moreover, Asoka urged people to propagate the *dharma*. "Relatives should propagate (the teaching) appropriately to their own relative." He saw to it that the edicts were recited on fixed days and that their purport was clarified. "This document should be heard on the Tishya day every for-monthly season; and, indeed, on every festive occasion in between the Tishya days it may be heard even by one (official). By acting thus, endeavor to fulfill (my instructions)." But, in the case of Asoka, any intention of emphasizing the prestige of the monarch from his quality as a sovereign is not found. His words were claimed to be esteemed for the reason that they expressed universal laws. Nor in the Sixteen-Article Law of Songtsan-Gampo is loyalty to the monarch taught at all.

What *was* stressed by Prince Shōtoku, however, was the relation between lord (emperor), officials, and the common people in the centralized state.

Officials rule common people in compliance with the command of the emperor. The principle of governing the state is propriety, moral or morality in a wider sense. If the superiors are lacking in morality, the common people cannot be ruled; if the common people are lacking in morality, many crimes and delinquencies will happen, however much an endeavor may be made. Management by officials should therefore be based upon propriety or morality.

The relationship between the emperor, the officials, and the common people was expressed after the model of ancient China, formulated in State Confucianism, but implanted on the soil of Japan. It seems that this conception was closely connected with the abolition of ownership of land and people by big clans on the occasion of the Taika Innovation.

This development firmly established the basis for the Emperor Institution.

The thought of esteeming the prestige of the emperor is especially conspicuous in the Constitution. "Provincial governors and district administrators should not levy exacting taxes on their respective peoples. In a country there should not be two lords; the people should not have two masters. The people of the whole country have the Sovereign as their sole master. The officials appointed to administer the local affairs are all his subjects. How can they levy arbitrary taxes on the people in the manner of public administration?" (Article XII) This Article is assumed to bespeak the centralized administration in the territory under the Imperial Court, and to presage the abolishment of ownership of land and people which occurred later on a nation-wide scale; the rights and power entrusted to officials were going to diminish. The preceding clauses of Article XII also herald the absolutism of the later Emperor Institution, which was characteristic of Japan. Such a way of esteeming the prestige of the Emperor can hardly be illustrated from the abundant classical literature of India and China; while in the West, where Christianity was the predominant factor, it would also be difficult to find a counterpart.

To quote from Professor NORTHROP: "Admiral PERRY confronted the Japanese leaders with Western nationalism and the power of modern Western military weapons. Western nationalism requires, as its name suggests, primary loyalty to the nation rather than to the Asian joint family. Shintoism contributed exactly this. For it is of the essence of Shintoism that the Japanese people are the descendants of a sun goddess."[24]

The ultimate form in which the Japanese concept of emphasis upon a specific, limited human nexus manifested itself was ultranationalism, which appeared after the Meiji Restoration. But Japanese ultra-nationalism did not suddenly appear in the post-Meiji period; its beginning can be traced to the very remote past.

The notion of Japanese superiority is most boldly expressed in the concept of the Divine Nation. We find the following statement by KITA-BATAKE Chikafusa, a Shintoist writer (1293–1354): "Our Great Nippon is a Divine Nation. Our Divine Ancestors founded it; the Sun Goddess let her descendants reign over it for a long time. This is unique to Our Nation; no other nation has the like of it. This is the reason why Our Nation is called a 'Divine Nation.' "[25] This concept of a "Divine Nation" was adopted by some Buddhists, such as the Nichiren and Zen masters.

Confucianism, which the Chinese had earlier adopted as their official theory of the state, was accepted by the Japanese with hardly any trouble. (The only controversial point was the problem of changing un-suitable emperors; even this, however, caused no special friction.) When Confucianism was introduced into Japan, the ruling class studied it so that they could "become government officials and Confucians, and serve the country."[26]

This attitude toward Confucianism was to persist among the ruling classes, and in the Tokugawa period Confucianism was taught with special reference to the concept of the state (*kokutai*) by almost all the schools and individual scholars of Confucianism including ITŌ Jinsai, YAMAGA Sokō, YAMAZAKI Ansai, and the Mito school. Japanese Con-fucianism, associated with the nationalism or the authority-conscious-ness of the Japanese people, asserted its own superiority over foreign systems of thought.

But since the Confucian concept of the state was formulated in accord-ance with the needs of Chinese society, it naturally contained a number of principles with which the more thorough-going Japanese nationalists could not agree. The state as conceived by Chinese philosophers was an idealistic model state; while the state that the Japanese nationalists had in mind was the actual Japanese state. This was the reason that Japanese nationalism—nurtured, so to speak, by Confucianism—had ultimately to deny the authority of Confucianism. YOSHIDA Shōin, the most influ-ential leader of the movement to establish the modern state of Japan, declared in his criticism of CONFUCIUS and MENCIUS: "It was wrong of CONFUCIUS and MENCIUS to have left their native states and to have served other countries, for a sovereign and a father are essentially the same. To call one's sovereign unwise and dull, and forsake one's native state in order to find another sovereign in another state, is like calling one's father foolish and moving from one's house to the next house to become the son of a neighbor. That CONFUCIUS and MENCIUS lost sight of this truth can never be justified."[27]

A similar tendency can easily be discerned in the process of assimilation of Buddhism. Japanese Buddhists carefully picked out such doctrines as would be convenient for, or not inconsistent with, their nationalism.

The *Suvarpaprabhāse-sūtra* and some later scriptures of Mahāyāna Buddhism, unlike those of early Buddhism, advance the theory that a monarch is a son of divine beings (*tenshi, devaputra*) to whom has been given a mandate from Heaven, and whom Heaven will protect. This theory, which became greatly cherished in Japan, had its origin in the Brahmin law-books, which regulated the feudal society of medieval India. Later, Indian Buddhists came to mention this theory merely as a prevailing notion of society. Although not characteristic of Buddhism, this idea came to be especially stressed by the Japanese.

The attitude which Indian Buddhism assumed toward the state was, from the time of its origination, one of caution. For instance, it placed monarchs in the same category with robbers; both were thought to endanger people's welfare. According to Buddhist legend, the people in remote antiquity elected a common head who would see to it that the people were protected, good people rewarded, evil people punished. The sovereign originated from this (*cf.* social contract). The Buddha Sākyamuni is said to have praised the republic of the Vajjis as the ideal state form.

But the Japanese, who accepted Buddhism on a large scale, refused nevertheless to adopt its concept of the state which to them appeared to run counter to the native idea of "state structure" (*kakutai*). We thus had a writer named KITABATAKE Chikafusa who was ready, on the one hand, to accept Buddhism in general, but eager, on the other, to emphasize the importance of the Japanese Imperial Family in the following way: "The Buddhist theory (of the state) is merely an Indian theory; Indian monarchs may have been the descendants of a monarch selected for the people's welfare, but our Imperial Family is the only continuous and unending line of family descending from its Heavenly Ancestors."[28]

HIRATA Atsutane, a fanatic Shintoist leader, discredits the whole Indian theory of the origin of the state as a mere explanation of the origin of "Indian chieftains."[29]

It is evident from the references in historical documents to the purpose of the adoption of Buddhism that considerations of protection for the state by means of prayers and religious rites constituted a dominant factor in Japanese Buddhism from the very beginning. Most Japanese monasteries in those early days were state-operated. Protection of the state, a prime concern in the Japanese mind, was thus firmly established in religion, and became the slogan of nearly all the Buddhist sects.

So far we have dealt with the problem of nationalism from the viewpoint of philosophy and religion. The outstanding features of Japanese nationalism may be summed up as follows:

In the past, the Japanese people dedicated a large and important part of their individual life to the state—to an extent never attempted by other Eastern peoples. The extent of such dedication is itself the first feature of Japanese nationalism.

The second feature is that Japanese nationalism was developed from concern for the particular state of Japan. There are different ways in which nationalism is applied in practice: We know that it has, many times, been expounded by thinkers in India and China, as well as in the West. But their nationalism was theoretically concerned with the state in general, and not with their particular state. Nationalism tends, by its very nature, to be applied to a state in particular. In Japanese nationalism, by way of contrast with the above-mentioned states, the particular entity of Japan came to be the sole standard upon which all judgments were based. This fact, without doubt, hashed a close relationship with the general tendency in Japanese thinking, especially in the past, to overlook the universal and to lay stress upon an exclusive human nexus. In the opinion of this writer, the natural basis for Japan's exclusive concern with herself is isolated from the continent by water. The Japanese have only rarely experienced a real fear of alien peoples; they have known the existence of foreign nations only indirectly, except in the case of World War II.

The dominance of the state over individual life was, in a sense, a condition extremely favorable to Japan's start as a modern state, if only in form, in the Meiji era. One imagines that it would have been difficult for her to become the modern state that she is today so quickly, had it not been for the strong consciousness the people have had for the state. As the modern history of the West has shown, the formation of the state is a necessary condition for the active progress of peoples. Japan, in this sense, may be said to have been more favorably conditioned for modernization than other nations of the East which were not so unified.

Certain apprehension may, however, be felt here by some. They may ask: Is not Japan's state-consciousness already a thing of the past? Is she not being rapidly modernized? Has not the experience of defeat in World War II brought the Japanese people to consider themselves as individuals making up their society and participating in the sovereignty of the state, rather than "subjects" of the Emperor?

We are inclined to offer only a tentative "yes" to these questions. For, although it is true that changes are being made in these directions, it is also true that it is no easy task for the Japanese to do away with their inherent thinking. We must remember that the country is overflowing with people, with a network of tightlyformed village communities covering the land. The nation's economy is such that the state must still exercise controls over a large portion of individual life. Above all, since distant antiquity the nation's progress has always had its motivation in the Imperial Family, although it is now not so powerful as before. Furthermore, the Japanese sentiment toward the Imperial House has been friendly rather than hostile, as in some other foreign countries, and the ruling class were often quite benevolent in their dealings with the people. All in all, an atmosphere of family-like intimacy pervaded by Westerners, and even by Indians or Chinese, as self-contradictory. The Japanese, however, felt no inconsistency in the term, but found it good and valid. In view of these factors, would it really be possible to put an end to the Japanese way of thinking about the State? This is not something we can take pride in before other nations; but, just as religion was the basis of the practical morals of the Chinese, so the state was the basis of all thought among the Japanese.[30] The Japanese way of thinking is undergoing a change, but their thinking is an inheritance, a tradition. We feel that it is our part to see to it that this tradition never again gives rise to an inhuman ultranationalism, but to a world-wide solidarity in the future.

Economic Activities in This-Worldly Life

It is a problem worthy of study why the Japanese alone among the many Asiatic countries came to be far advanced several decades ago in adopting modern civilization. In respect to this, we should like to point out the emphasis upon social activities as one of the features of the Japanese way of thinking. This feature can be traced back even to the thought of Prince Shōtoku.

The phenomenalistic way of thinking that asserts reality itself to be emergent and in flux has been traditionally prevalent among Japanese. This emergent and fluid way of thinking is compatible with the inclination of thinking that emphasizes a particular human nexus—another way of thinking which is traditionally conspicuous among Japanese. These two factors have combined to bring about an emphasis upon activities within a concrete human nexus.

It is a well-known fact that primitive Shintoism was closely tied up with agricultural rituals in agrarian villages, and that Shintoist gods have been symbolized, till now, as gods of production.

Coming into contact with foreign cultures and becoming acquainted with Chinese philosophies and religions, the Japanese adopted and absorbed Confucianism in particular, which teaches a way of conduct appropriate to a concrete human nexus. The thoughts of LAO Tzu and CHUANG Tzu are inclined to a life of seclusion in which one escapes from a particular human nexus and seeks tranquility in solitude. Such was not to the taste of the Japanese at large. In contrast, Confucianism principally determines rules of conduct according to a system of human relationships. In this respect, Confucianism never came in conflict with the existing Japanese thought patterns at the time of implantation.

In the case of Buddhism, however, some problems arose. Buddhism declared itself to be a teaching of other-worldliness. According to Buddhist philosophy, the positive state of "other-worldliness" is arrived at after one has transcended "this world." The central figures in Buddhist orders have all been monks and nuns, who have freed themselves not only from their families but from any specific human nexus. They were not allowed to become involved in any economic or worldly activities. It is likely that in olden days there existed social reasons that prompted a great many people to become monks.

In addition, the topographical characteristics of Japan, vastly different from India, require men to serve humanity within a specific human nexus. The doctrine of early Buddhism was not compatible with such requirements, so early Buddhism and traditional conservative Buddhism, which inherited the former teachings, were despised and rejected under the name of Hinayāna, and Mahāyāna Buddhism was particularly favored and adopted. Mahāyāna Buddhism was a popular religion that came to the fore after the Christian Era. Some schools of Mahāyāna Buddhism, if not all, advocated the finding of the absolute truth within secular life. In accepting Buddhism, the Japanese selected in particular the form which had such characteristics; even in accepting those doctrines which were originally devoid of this nature, they deliberately bestowed such a character upon them. The stereotyped phrase, "Japan is the country where Mahāyāna Buddhism is practiced,"[31] can be understood solely by reference to these basic facts.

Such an attitude in accepting Buddhism is clearly shown in the case of Prince Shōtoku. His "Commentaries upon Three Sūtras" are those upon the *Shōman (Srimaladevisimhanada)-sūtra,* the *Yuima (Vimalakirtinirdesa)-sūtra,* and the *Lotus (Saddharmapundarika)-sūtra.* The selection of these three Sūtras out of a multitude was entirely based upon the Japanese way of thinking. The *Shōman Sūtra* was preached, in compliance with Buddha's command, by Madame Shōman (Srimāllā), who was the queen and a lay believer. The *Yuima Sūtra* has a dramatic composition, in which *Yuima (Vimalakirti),* lay believers, reversed the usual order and give sermons to *priests and ascetics.* In the first two *sūtras,* they commend the idea of grasping the truth in secular life; while, according to the last, all laymen who faithfully follow any of the teachings of Buddha are expected to be redeemed.

The Crown Prince himself, all through his life, remained a lay believer. It is said that he called himself "*Shōman, the Child of a Buddha.*"[32] The intention of Prince Shōtoku was to place emphasis upon the realization of Buddhist ideals within the concrete human nexus of people retaining in secular life. He sought absolute significance within the practical conduct of everyday life, and asserted: "Reality is no more than today's occurrence of cause and effect." He added: "Ten thousand virtues are all contained in today's effect."[33] Such an interpretation has something in common with the doctrine of the Tendai and Kegon sects, but the particular expression "today's" makes it distinctly Japanese. For those who have gone through Buddhist reflection, this world of impurities and sufferings in itself turns out to be a place of blessings, as the doctrine attaches great importance to action. "Since I wish to enlighten mankind, I regard life and death as a garden."[34] All the good deeds practised in the world of life and death are eventually turned into the causes that lead men into the rank of a Buddha. "Uncountable ten thousand good deeds equally lead to becoming a Buddha."[35]

It is worth noting that the ultimate state of religion is not bestowed upon men by divine entities that transcend them, but is realized through practice within the human nexus. "The result of becoming a Buddha originates from ten thousand good deeds."[36] Mahāyāna Buddhism stressed altruistic deeds; Prince Shōtoku assigned special emphasis to them and considered that Buddhas and Bodhisattvas should serve all living beings. That is the reason for occasional distorted interpretations given to phrases in the Buddhist scriptures.[37] According to the Lotus Sūtra the advice is given "to sit always in religious meditation." This sentence was revised by Prince Shōtoku to mean: "Do not approach a person who always sits in religious meditation."[38] The meaning is that unintermittent sitting in meditation enables a man to practice altruistic deeds.

A similar idea underlies the later teachings of Japanese Buddhism. According to Saichō (Master Dengyō), both priests and laymen attain the self-same ideal (the consistency of clergy and laity). According to Kūkai (Master Kōbō), the founder of Japanese Vajrayāna, absolute reason should be realized through actuality. (Reality is revealed in accordance with phenomenal things.) "Pure Land" Buddhism also developed along that line. The idea that he who believes in the true wish of Amitābha will be redeemed, staying as he is in a lay condition, persisted through all the later periods. The Jōdo Shin Sect emphasized not only that all living creatures are saved on account of their religious faith (the turning towards the Pure Land), but also that the Great Benevolence saves all those who are lost (the returning from the Pure Land). During the Tokugawa period, the most famous itinerant merchants of Ōmi Province, who peddled assiduously all around the country, were devoted followers of the Jōdo Shin Sect who travelled with the spirit of service to others.

Buddhist morals were also metamorphosed. The Indians considered alms-giving, a virtue of principal importance for Buddhists, as something to be strictly observed. Most of the Buddhist scriptures extol the deeds of those who abandoned not only their country, castle, wives and children, but also their own bodies, and gave most generously to other human beings (or even to animals).[39] Such a life of abandoning everything and possessing nothing was an ideal life for the Indian ascetics. Recourse to such drastic measures, however, was not allowed for the Japanese, who attached more importance to the concrete human nexus. Prince Shōtoku, therefore, confine the meaning of "alms-giving" to "the abandonment of properties other than one's own body."[40] In this manner, the inclination of the Indians to go imaginatively beyond the ethics of the mundane human relationship underwent a revision when Buddhism was accepted by the Japanese.

The emphasis upon the human nexus ran parallel to the stress upon all the productive activities of men. In a country like India, where the intensity of heat, the abundance of seasonal rainfall, and the fertility of the soil together bring forth a rich harvest, without much human labor needing to be exerted on the land, the ethics of distribution rather than of production are naturally emphasized. That is a reason why alms-giving comes to be considered most important. But in a country like Japan, by way of contrast, production is of vital importance; hence stress is placed upon the ethics of labor in the various professions.

The Lotus Sūtra, the most important of all the Japanese Buddhist scriptures, was accepted by the Japanese as something that gives a theoretical basis for such a social and economic demand.

This sūtra states that, if one preaches with comprehension of the true purport of the Lotus Sūtra. "When one preaches various teachings, they all coincide with the true purport and nothing will contradict the True Aspect of Reality. When one elucidates secular treaties, the words of this-worldly government, or the deeds of production, they all accord with the True Doctrine."[41] This sentence was interpreted by the Japanese to mean that everything is true as long as it comes from a man who has once comprehended the truth of Lotus Sūtra. The same sentence was further interpreted by the Japanese, however, to mean that all activities in the fields of politics and economics were to be subjected to the Absolute One. Shōsui Shiei explained the sentence thus: "The One Mind, the Eternal Truth, and the aspect of appearance and disappearance are no separate things. That they are one is revealed in accordance with that they are three; that they are three is discussed in accordance with that they are one. Government and production, therefore, could be in no contradiction to the True Aspect of Reality."[42] This idea of Shōsui came to be taken by the Japanese to be the original idea of the Lotus Sūtra.

Government and production, therefore, could not be in contradiction with the True Aspect of Reality. Some Japanese Buddhists were thus led to recognize the particularly sacred significance of physical labor. It is an historically well-known fact that the Buddhists endeavored to go directly to the people through various welfare activities.

This feature can be noticed even in Japanese Zen literature. Dōgen, the founder of Sōtō Zen, thought that Buddhism could be realized within the professional lives of the secular society. SUZUKI Shōsan, a Zen master, found absolute significance in the pursuit of one's own profession, whether warrior, farmer, craftsman, merchant, doctor, actor, hunter, or priest. Because it is the essence of Buddhism, according to him, to rely

upon the original self or upon "the true Buddha of one's own," and because every profession is the function of this "One Buddha," it amounts
to the fact that to pursue one's own profession is to obey the Absolute
One. So he teaches farmers: "Farming is nothing but the doings of
Buddha." To merchants he teaches: "Renounce desires and pursue profits single-heartedly. But you should never enjoy profits. You should,
instead, work for the good of all the others." Since the afflictions of this
world, it is said, are predetermined in former lives, one should torture
oneself by working hard in one's own profession, in order to redeem the
sins of the past. It is noteworthy that immediately after the death of
CALVIN, an idea similar to his happened almost contemporaneously to
appear in Japan. The fact, however, that it never grew into a capitalistic
movement of great consequence ought to be studied in relation to the
underdevelopment of the modern bourgeois society in Japan.

Such a theory of religion also leds itself to religious movements outside of Buddhism in Japan. To illustrate, NINOMIYA Sontoku's movement inclines to be practical and activistic. Sectarian Shintoism assumes
a similar tendency. The founder of the Tenri religion teaches: "Keep
your heart pure, busy yourself with your profession, and be true to the
mind of God." The other new sects of Shintoism mostly fall into a
similar pattern.

Respect for labor in professional life resulted in high esteem for things
produced as the fruits of labor. Reverence for foodstuffs is especially
manifest. Dōgen, the Zen master, for example, recognizes the sacred
significance of food and says that each item of foodstuffs should be
labelled with honorifics. The tendency to teach the taking of good care
of all the products of labor, however trivial they might be, is also manifest among the Jōdo Shin Sect, which is diametrically opposed, in other
respects, to Zen Buddhism.

The precept that we should take good care of economic products, the
fruits of human labor, is not necessarily confined to Japanese religions
only, but seems common to most universal religions. In India or South
Asian countries, however—where men are not required to labor too
hard in order to produce daily necessities—relatively little has been said

against waste. The fact that the preservation of economic products is particularly emphasized should be considered in the light of the topological peculiarity of Japan.

The form in which Chinese thought was accepted was also tinged with an activist tendency in interpreting the ways of human beings. ITŌ Jinsai (1627–1705), in particular, understood what is called the Way as being active and as representing the principle of growth and development. On that basis he rejected the nihilism of LAO Tzu. OGYŪ Sorai (1666–1728), a peculiarly Japanese Confucianist, positively advocated activism, rejecting the static tendency of the Confucianists of the Sun period of China. Quiet sitting, with reverential love in one's heart, was the method of mental training extolled by the Confucianists of that period, which was thus ridiculed by Sorai: "As I look at them, even gambling appears superior to quiet sitting and having reverential love in one's heart." A necessary conclusion drawn from such an attitude was the recommendation, as made by Sorai, of practical learning, useful in practical life. Such was the mental climate which nurtured the economic theory of DAZAI Shundai and the legal philosophy of MIURA Chikkei. Whereas Chinese Confucianism surpassed Japanese Confucianism in thinking upon metaphysical problems, Japanese Confucianism directed its attention to politics, economics, and law—the practical aspects of human life.

That Japan alone made rapid progress in modernization during the years just before World War II, while the other Asian countries were generally slow in this process, may be attributed partly to the emphasis laid by the Japanese upon practical activities within the human nexus.

A great danger lies in the fact that the religious view of the Japanese may easily degenerate into the sheer utilitarianism of profit-seeking activities, in case it loses sight of the significance of the absolute, which underlies the productive life of professions. But at the same time credit should be given to the tendency to esteem the human nexus. If the religion of Japan is enhanced to such a height that religious truth may be realized in accordance with the human nexus (which is at once universal and particular, transcending every specific nexus and at the same time embracing all of them), then and only then will it achieve universal significance.

2. Buddhist Influence upon Japanese Ways of Thinking

Introductory Remarks

It is a well-known fact that Japanese thought in general has been greatly influenced by Buddhism. Buddhist philosophy itself is an elaborate system of thought, and the traces of its influence upon the Japanese can be found in many aspects of their life. For thorough investigation of all of them, even a life-time would scarcely be enough. Now as a humble student of Indian and Buddhist thought, I should like to discuss some features of the Japanese way of thinking related to Buddhist thinking.

Rennyo, a great propagator of Pure Realm Buddhism, said: "It was in the reign of Emperor Kimmei that the Buddhist Gospel was introduced into our country. Before that time the teaching of Buddhism was not propagated here, and there was nobody who attained enlightenment. Due to some good causes (i.e., merits) in the past lives, we have had the fortune to be born in a time when Buddhism is flourishing, and good to hearken to the teaching for salvation."[43]

There are so many traces of Buddhist influence upon the Japanese way of thinking. In the following, three conspicuous features will be discussed.

1) humanitarianism
2) moral self-reflection
3) tolerance.

Humanitarianism

The problem of humanitarianism has been discussed by many scholars from different points of view. I should like to add some comments upon this problem from the standpoint of a student of Indian and Buddhist philosophy.

As one of the most prominent features of Japanese ways of thinking, we may point out the emphasis on the love of human beings.

In ancient Japan a man asked a Zen priest: "The sūtra says one could not be a Bodhisattva[44] unless one serves Buddhas by burning one's own body, elbows, and fingers. What is the meaning of this?" Answer: "The burning of one's body, elbows, and fingers is metaphorically used to mean the elimination of the three sorts of ignorance, of the branch, the leaf, and the root. . . . If one eliminates these three darknesses, one becomes a Bodhisattva. . . . If one should try to serve the Buddhas by burning one's actual body, would any Buddha receive it?" Here the practices actually followed among the Buddhists both in ancient India and China were completely denied by the Japanese Buddhists.

The Japanese put special emphasis upon the love of others. Among many sects of Japanese Buddhism, the Pure Land Buddhism (Jōdo Sect) a religion which typically emphasizes benevolence, enjoys great popularity. The Pure Land Buddhism preaches the benevolence of Amitābha Buddha, who saves even bad men and ordinary men. Most of the high priests of the sect have especially benign looks. The emphasis upon the deeds of benevolence is recognizable also in other sects. The Japanese accepted the practice of the strict disciplines handed down from primitive Buddhism in the form of the "Ritsu Sect." This sect originally followed a seclusionist method of ascetic practices. Later, however, with its development into the Shingon-Ritsu sect, a priest like Ninshō (1217–1303) launched upon such social welfare works as helping the suffering and the sick. He dedicated his whole life to the service of others. For this he was even criticized by his master, "he overdid benevolence." It was a breach of the ancient disciplines to dig ponds or wells or to give medicine and clothing to the sick or to accumulate money for them, but he never let himself be influenced by this.

Needless to say, the idea of benevolence had an important significance in Chinese Buddhism. Zen Buddhism, however, developed as a Chinese people's Buddhism, did not seem to emphasize the idea of benevolence so much. To confirm this, there is not a single reference made to the word "benevolence" in such well-known scriptures as "Shin-jin-mei" (the Epigram of Faith), "Shodo-ka" (the Song of Enlightenment), "Sandō-

kai" (Compliance with the Truth), and *"Hōkyozammai"* (Precious-Mirror Mediation). To go back still further, nothing is said about it in what is supposed to be the teachings of Bodhidharma.[45] It is probable that the Chinese Zen sect, under the influence of Taoism and other traditional ideologies of China, was inclined to seclusion and resignation, and neglected the positive approach of practicing deeds of benevolence. Such is my general impression, though a final conclusion cannot be drawn until we have made a thorough study of the general history of the Chinese Zen sect. At the time the Zen sect was brought into Japan, however, it came to emphasize deeds of benevolence, just as the other sects in Japan did. Eisai, who introduced Rinzai-Zen, put the idea of benevolence to the forefront. In a reply to the question whether the Zen sect was not too much obsessed by the idea of the void, he says: "To prevent by means of self-discipline the evil from without and to profit others with benevolence within—this is what Zen is." As for the rules for ascetics of the Zen sect, he teaches: "You should arouse the spirit of great benevolence—and save mankind with the pure and supreme disciplines of the Great Bodhisattva, but you ought not to seek deliverance for your own sake." SOSEKI (MUSŌ Kokushi), SUZUKI Shōsan, Shidō Munan, and other Zen priests represent a positive repulsion against the seclusionist and self-satisfied attitude of the traditional Zen sect. They stress, instead the virtue of "benevolence" overtly, chooses for instruction the phrase, "speak kingly to others" (words of affection) from among the various Buddhist doctrines of the past. "Speaking words of affection means to generate the heart of benevolence and bestow upon others the language of affection, whenever one sees them. To speak with the heart, looking at mankind with benevolence as though they were your own children, is to utter words of affection. The virtuous should be praised, the virtueless pitied. To cause the enemy to surrender, or to make the wise yield, words of affection are most fundamental. To hear words of affection in one's presence brightens one's countenance and warms one's heart. To hear words of affection said in one's absence goes home to one's heart and soul. You should learn to know that words of affection are powerful enough to set a river on fire." In addition, he puts emphasis upon the virtues of giving, altruism and collaboration, at the bottom of which flows the pure current of affection.

The spirit of benevolence was not only preached by Buddhists, but it also made its way into Shintoism, and tied up with one of the three divine symbols of the Japanese Imperial Family. It also was popularized among the general public and came to be regarded as one of the principal virtues of the *samurai*. The love of others by no means comes out of self-complacency. On the contrary, it goes with a humble reflection that I, as well as others, am an ordinary man. This had already been stressed by Prince Shōtoku at the beginning of the introduction of Buddhism into Japan.

"Forget resentment, forsake anger, do not become angry just because someone opposes you. Everyone has a mind, every mind comes to a decision, and decisions will not always be alike. If he is right, you are wrong; if you are right, he is wrong; if you are not quite a saint, he is not quite an idiot. Both disputants are men of ordinary mind; who is decisively capable of judging an argument between them? If both are wise men or both foolish men their argument is probably a vicious circle. For this reason, if your opponent grows angry, you had better be all the more cautious lest you too are in error. Although you might think you are quite right, it is wiser to comply with the other man." (The Precepts of Prince Shōtoku X) Out of this emerged the spirit of tolerance, which we shall discuss later.

The problem remain whether or not this tendency to stress love is inherent to the Japanese people. That there is no god of love in Shintoism was once criticised by a famous Buddhist scholar, caused a great sensation among the Shintoists. They presented some counter-evidence, which seemed far from convincing. This issue cannot be settled as yet, but requires further investigation. But the general impression is that the spirit of benevolence was introduced into Japan probably with the advent of Buddhism and exerted a renovating influence upon the mental attitude of the Japanese. Within this limit, it may be asserted that there exists a certain element of humanitarianism in the thinking of the common man in Japan.

Moral Self-Reflection

The second conspicuous feature of Buddhist influence upon Japanese ways of thinking is the acuteness of moral self-reflection. I do not mean that the Japanese are more keen on moral problems than other nations, but that the moral attitude of the Japanese is to a great extent due to Buddhist influence.

In pre-Buddhist Japan people rejoiced in this-worldly life without acute self-reflection. Their actions were aimed at physical or sensual pleasures. Princes held frequent festivals; they became easily intoxicated with liquor. They composed love songs in a joyful mood. They were rather passionate. Incest was prevalent throughout the people. They were enjoying happy days simple-mindedly just like children. Sins were regarded as something material. The ancient Japanese thought that they had only to get rid of them by means of simple practices of religious or physical purifications (e.g. invocation of formulae, ablution, etc.)

The advent of Buddhism caused the Japanese to open their mental eye to the spiritual or metaphysical realm. Owing to Buddhist influences, the Japanese in general have come to hold the notion that good deeds (merits) bring forth good results, just as in the Western proverb: "Sow virtue, and the harvest will be virtue."

The consciousness of sin came to be most conspicuous in the case of St. Shinran.

Pure Land (Realm) Buddhism, introduced from China, reached the zenith of its development with Shinran, in whom the working of moral self-reflection was extremely strong. "Truly I have come to realize, and it is deplorable, that I, an idiotic vulture, am drowned in the boundless sea of carnal desire, lost in the enormous mountains of worldly ambitions, not being pleased with becoming entitled to be saved, and taking no pleasure in approaching the True Evidence. Shame on me; woe is me!" Moral self-reflection as acute as Shinran's seems not to be shown in the Buddhist literature of other countries. Monks who broke their vows in India appear to have held the notion that sins could be expiated by reciting magical formulae *(dhāranī)*. Little has been said about the pangs of conscience of renegade monks in China either. Shinran, on the contrary, could not but face the shameful reality of man. Shinran, who looked into the deeper self of man, turned to the Buddha, the absolute one. He was thus led to advocate "the discipline of non-discipline," which was based on self-reflection of great moral intensity.

The motivation for the ascetics of India and China to enter the priesthood was, in most cases, the realization of the impermanence of the phenomenal world rather than the realization of man's sinfulness. In the case of Shinran, in contrast, little is said about the impermanence of this world. The controlling motivation for Shinran is the sense of the sinfulness of man. It is not that man is simply changeful. A more fundamental thing about man is that he is a sinner, obsessed with afflictions, yielding to evils. Realizing as he does that things are impermanent, he still clutches at these impermanent things. Man is so deeply immersed in sins that he could never be saved but for the miraculous power of the vow of Amitābha. Such was Shinran's doctrine.

It is noteworthy that profound religious self-reflection, based upon the Pure Realm doctrine, was professed by some of the emperors.

"Though the mind's moon shines
To show the way to the Pure Land,
Woe be to the clouds still uncleansed." (By Emperor Gotoba)

This poem means that ardent as my desire is to be reborn into the Pure Realm trusting and relying upon the vow of Amitābha, the sins I have committed weigh so heavily upon my heart that I am haunted by doubts about the vows; and how far beyond comprehension, the poem laments, is the state of the salvation.

Religious and moral self-reflection as profound as that stated above is not confined to Japanese Pure Realm Buddhism. The form of accepting the Zen doctrine in Japan, as in the case of Dōgen, reveals a profound moral self-reflection. He attaches great importance to the act of making confession. "Should you confess in this manner, the assistance of the Buddha will assuredly be yours. Make a confession to the Buddha with your soul and body and the power of the confession will eradicate all the roots of your sins." He commends good deeds, and preaches that one will be able to become a Buddha through one's good acts. "Quite an easy way there is to become a Buddha. Not to do evil deeds, not to be obsessed with the matter of life and death, but to take pity upon mankind, to revere the gods, to be considerate to inferiors, and to keep one's mind free from hatred, desires, afflictions and anxieties is exactly what is called being a Buddha. One should not seek Buddhahood anywhere else." He emphasizes the observance of injunctions.

The emphasis upon the introspection among Japanese priests, is apparent also among laymen. For example, MINAMOTO Sanetomo, the medieval feudal lord, says:

> "There's no way out
> Of this agonizing hell,
> Whose empty vault
> Only flames can fill.
> The founder of a temple,
> The erector of a tower,
> For their acts get credit;
> But none gets merits
> So rewarding as a repentant sinner."

On the whole, when and only when one reflects upon one's deeds sincerely enough, is one awakened to one's sinfulness.

It was also reported by the European missionaries who came to Japan at the early stage of the modern period, that crimes were relatively few, and reason reigned among the Japanese.

In any case, although they may be weak in sin-consciousness in its religious sense, the Japanese are sensitive in shame-consciousness in its practical and moral sense.

For the Japanese in general, whether or not one infringes religious disciplines is a matter of little consequence. A matter of vital importance for them is whether or not one conforms to the morals of the particular human nexus to which one belongs.

The listing of virtues after the fashion of Indian Buddhism, however, was not to the liking of the Japanese in general, who looked for the one central virtue directly posited. It is the virtue of "*honesty* (sincerity)," which was originally adopted from Buddhism, that emerged from such a demand, and come to be generally recognized as the central virtue by the Japanese. Ancient imperial rescripts state: "the honest heart to be the virtue that all the subjects should observe." Probably influenced by them was the doctrine of the Ise Shrine, according to which the Sun Goddess was supposed to have said: "Divine protection is based upon honesty." During the Muromachi period, the virtue of "honesty" as the doctrine of the Ise Shrine came to prevail among the entire country. It was generally recognized by the Japanese of those days that the virtue of "honesty" in Shintoism originated from Buddhism.

Tolerance

The Japanese are said to be distinguished from other ancient nations by their spirit of tolerance. Although there must have been interracial conflicts in prehistoric Japan, there exists no evidence, as far as archaeological remains are concerned, that their armed conflicts were too violent. According to the classical records also, the Japanese treated the other peoples, whom they had conquered, with the spirit of tolerance. As for tales of wars there are many, but there is no evidence that the conquered peoples were made into slaves *in toto*. Even the prisoners were not treated as slaves in the Western sense of the word. Although there remains some doubt as to whether or not there existed a so-called slave-economy in ancient Japan, since the percentage of slave-servants was very small in the whole population, it may be safely said that the labor-power of the slaves was never used on a large scale. Such a social condition gives rise to the tendency to stress the dominance-control-by-power relationship. This is not to deny entirely the presence of the latter type of relationship in the Japanese society since olden days. The social restrictions and pressure upon the individual might have been indeed stronger than in many other countries. Nevertheless, in the consciousness of each individual Japanese, the spirit of conciliation (harmony) and tolerance is preeminent.

The spirit of tolerance of the Japanese made it impossible to cultivate deep hatred even toward sinners. In Japan there existed hardly any punishment that was cruel. Since crucifixion appeared for the first time in Japanese history during the age of civil wars, it was presumably started after the advent of Christianity, and suggested by it. Burning at the stake seemed to be in practice during the reign of Emperor Yuryaku, but it went out of practice afterwards to be revived occasionally during the modern period.

In the medieval West, condemnation at the stake took place under religious authority, which never happened in Japan. During the Heian period, capital punishment was not practiced for three hundred and fifty years. It was not revived until the War of Hogen took place. Although this may be attributed to the influence of Buddhism, there has hardly been any period in any other country marked with the absence of the death penalty.

For the Japanese, full of the spirit of tolerance, eternal damnation is absolutely inconceivable. A Catholic priest, who forsook Christianity under the persecution of the Tokugawa Government, condemned the idea of eternal damnation preached in Christianity. He said, concerning rewards and punishments in the other world, that if God were the Lord of Benevolence, He ought to condemn Himself rather than condemn human beings and punish them for their sins. From among the doctrines of Christianity the idea of eternal damnation was especially hard for the Japanese to comprehend. Dr. ANESAKI M., commenting on this point, says: "This is the outstanding line of demarcation between Judaism and Buddhism." The Japanese also found it difficult to understand the idea of "being beyond deliverance for ever." The Hossō Sect, a school of Buddhist Idealism, based upon the philosophy of Dharmapāla, advocates "the difference of five predisposition." Among men there are five types, the man who is predisposed to become a Bodhisattva,[46] the one predisposed to become an *Enkaku* (pratyekabuddha, one who attains self-complacent enlightenment), one predisposed to become a *Shōmon* (srāvaka, and accetic of Hinayāna Buddhism), one who is not predisposed, and one who is beyond deliverance. Such an idea of discrimination was not generally accepted by the Japanese Buddhists. Prevalently accepted, instead, was the view, "All of mankind is predisposed to become Buddhas."

A question may be raised here. Is not the spirit of tolerance prominent among the Japanese an influence of Buddhism rather than an intrinsic native characteristic? Before the advent of Buddhism the Japanese also resorted to atrocities. Are not the Emperors Buretsu and Yūryaku described as violent and ruthless? The reason why the death penalty was not meted out during the Heian period was that the ideal of Buddhism was realized in politics.

Even in present-day Japan, statistics proves that in the districts where *haibutsu kishaku* (the abolition of Buddhism by violence immediately after the Meiji Restoration) was committed, cases of the murder of one's close relatives are high in number, whereas they are relatively low in number where Buddhism is vehemently supported. The reverse, however, may also be true, that because the Japanese were inherently tolerant and conciliatory, the infiltration of Buddhism into the people's lives was rapid. It is often pointed out by cultural historians that the Chinese people as a whole are inclined to ruthlessness and cruelty, in spite of the fact that the history of Buddhist influence in China is longer than it is in Japan. In Tibet, despite its being the country of Lamaism flying the banner of Buddhism, the severest of punishments are still in practice. So it may be concluded that the Japanese originally possessed the spirit of tolerance and forgiveness to some extent, which was much strengthened by the introduction of Buddhism, and was again weakened in recent years by the aggrandizement of the secular power on the one hand and by the decline of faith in Buddhism on the other. The fact that the Japanese are richly endowed with the spirit of tolerance and conciliation, while they are lacking in the intense hatred of sins, transformed the Pure Realm Buddhism. According to the eighteenth vow of Amitābha Buddha, he saves the whole of mankind on account of his great benevolence, the only exceptions being "those who committed five great sins and those who condemned the Right Law (Buddhism). Shan-tao (Zendō) of China interpreted this statement as meaning that even the great sinners, under the condition that they do converted, could be reborn into the Pure Land. Introduced into Japan, these exceptions were later considered as problematic, and came to be completely ignored by St. Hōnen. "This (salvation) includes all that are embraced in the great benevolence and the real vow of Amitābha, even the ten evils and five great sins not being excluded, and these who excel in those practices other than that of invocation of Amitābha being also included. Its meaning is to believe in what is revealed in the invocation of Amitābha for once and also for ten times." "You should believe that even those who have committed ten evils and five great sins are eligible for rebirth into the Pure Realm, and yet you should yourself refrain from the slightest of sins."

As far as the surface meaning of the sentence is concerned, Hōnen is diametrically opposed to the Indian men of religion who compiled the *Dai-mu-ryō-ju-kyō* (*Sukhāvativyūha-Sūtra*). Out of such an inclination of thinking was formulated the so-called "view of the eligibility of the evil ones for salvation" (the view that the evils are rightfully eligible for salvation by Amitābha Buddha). This may not be what Shinran really meant. But the fact that such a view was generally considered to be the fundamental doctrine of the Sin Sect can not be denied.

What are the rational basis for such a spirit of tolerance and conciliation? The tendency to recognize the absolute significance in everything phenomenal is conspicuous among the Japanese. It leads to the acceptance of the *raison d'etre* of any view held in the mundane world, and ends with the adjustment of any view with the spirit of tolerance and conciliation. Such a way of thinking appeared from the earliest days of the introduction of Buddhism into Japan. According to Prince Shōtoku, the Lotus Sūtra (The *Sadharmapundarika*-Sūtra), supposed to contain the ultimate essence of Buddhism, preaches the doctrine of the One Great Vehicle and advocates the theory "that any once of ten thousand goods leads to the one thing, the attainment of Enlightenment."

According to the Prince, there is no innate difference between saint and the most stupid men. Everyone is primarily and equally a saint and the most stupid man. Everyone is primarily and equally a child of the Buddha. Prince Shōtoku regarded the secular moral teachings as the elementary gate to enter Buddhism. His interpretation of Buddhism is characterized by its all-inclusive nature. Only by taking into consideration such a philosophical background is one able to understand the moral idea of the Prince when he says: "Concord is to be honored." It was this spirit that made possible the emergence of Japan as a unified cultural state. Prince Shōtoku's philosophical standpoint is represented by the expressions, "The One Great Vehicle" and "The Pure Great Vehicle," which are supposed to have originated from the Lotus Sūtra. Ever since Saichō (Master Dengyō) introduced the Tendai Sect, based upon the Hokke Sūtra, this sūtra has come to constitute the basis of Japanese Buddhism. Nichiren said "Japan is single-heartedly the country of the Lotus Sūtra," and "For more than four hundred years since Emperor Kammu, all the people of Japan have been single-heartedly devoted to the Lotus Sūtra." These words of Nichiren are not necessarily to be regarded as self-centered. Considering that the Pure Realm Buddhism and the Zen Sect even, not to mention the Nichiren Sect, are evidently under the influence of Tendai doctrine, there is much truth in these assertions of Nichiren. Among the poems composed on Buddhism by successive emperors, the subject matter is overwhelmingly on matters concerned with the Lotus Sūtra. The thought tendency characteristic of the Lotus Sūtra, which tried to accept the *raison d'être* of all the practices of Buddhism, led to an extremely tolerant and conciliatory attitude to various ideas.

Owing to such a spirit of tolerance and conciliation, the development on a single continuum of various sects was possible within Japanese Buddhism. In India today, there is no Buddhist tradition extant. In China uniformity was established in Buddhism; the Zen Sect fused with the Pure Realm Buddhism is the only remaining religious sect, whereas the traditions of all the rest of the sects almost went out of existence. In Japan, on the contrary, there still exist many traditional sects which can no longer be found in China or India.

In spite of the highly sectarian and factional tendency of the various religious sects keeping their traditional difference intact, the contempt of other sects was mutually prohibited by Japanese Buddhists. Even Rennyo of the Jōdo Shin Sect, which is supposed, to be inclined toward monotheistic Amidism and exclusionist, warns: "You ought not make light of shrines," and "You ought not slender other sects and other teachings."

SUZUKI Shōsan ordains: "In this monastery the right and wrong of the world or the relative merits of other sects ought not to be talked about." Jiun admonished his disciples: "The right and wrong or the high and low of the teachings of other sects should not be discussed."

Such an attitude of tolerance might have been handed down from Early Buddhism. It is noteworthy that, despite the sectarian and factional tendency of the Japanese, they did not want to dispute with their theoretical opponents. Realistically speaking, the amalgamation of Shintoism and Buddhism might have very well been an expedient measure taken in order to avoid friction between the traditional religion and the incoming Buddhism which came to be accepted as a national religion. It may also be said that it was a political consideration that made Hōnen and Rennyo warn against rejecting sects other than their own.

But the attitude of tolerance determined the all-inclusive and conciliatory nature of Japanese Buddhism. The ascendency of Buddhism in Japan in the course of more than ten centuries was entirely different from that of Christianity in the West. Buddhism tolerated various primitive faiths native to Japan. A clear notion of paganism was absent in Japanese Buddhism. The gods in the native Japanese popular religion, who should have been considered as pagan gods from the standpoint of Buddhism, were reconciled with Buddhism as temporary manifestations (incarnations avatāra) of the Buddha. Along this line of thought a theory called *honji-suijaku-setsu* was advanced, in which the Shintoist gods were maintained to be temporary incarnations of the Buddha. Emperor Yōmei is said to have "believed in Buddhism and at the same time to have worshipped the gods of Shintoism."

What "Shintoism" precisely means in the above question needs to be clarified, since in the Nara period the idea of the reconciliation of Shintoism and Buddhism had already come to the fore. According to this school of thought, the god rejoices in the Law of the Buddha and defends Buddhism, but since the god is an entirety in the mundane world just as other human beings are and is not free from affliction, he also seeks salvation. The Nara period saw many a shrine-temple built. The Imperial message of 767 stated that auspicious signs appeared, thanks to the

Buddha, the Japanese gods and goddesses of heaven and earth, and spirits of the successive emperors.

Thereafter, during the Heian period, there were few temples that did not have shrines built in their confines, where Buddhist priests performed the morning and evening practices of reciting sūtra, and served shrine of gods and goddesses together with Shintoist priests.

Indeed, deep-rooted was the belief among the common men in the native gods and goddesses was then enhanced to such an extent that they were entitled Bodhisattvas.

The gods and goddesses were thus exalted from the status of deluded mankind to that of persons who were on their way toward enlightenment, or to the status of those who save mankind.

The idea that the Japanese native gods are the temporary manifestations of the Buddha first appeared in the classical writings of the years of Kankō (1004–1012), in the middle of the Heian period. After the reign of Emperor Gosanjō, the question was raised as to what the fundamental basis was whose manifestations were these native gods and goddesses. During the period of the civil wars between the Genji and Heike clans, each god or goddess was gradually allotted to his or her own Buddha, whose incarnation he or she was supposed to be, until at last during the Shōkyū years (1218–1222), the idea was established that a god and the Buddha were identical in the body. "There is no difference between what is called a Buddha and what is called a god."

What is the way of thinking that made such a reconciliation of Buddhism and Shintoism possible? The influence of the traditional character of Buddhism cannot be denied, and it is particularly important to point out the influence of the idea of the One Vehicle manifested in the Lotus Sūtra. The Imperial Rescript of November, the third year of Shōwa (836) says: "There is nothing superior to the One Vehicle to defend Shintoism." It goes without saying that Nichiren, who expressed absolute allegiance to the Lotus Sūtra, also showed his genuine loyalty to the Japanese gods and goddesses. Even the Jōdo Shin Sect, which was originally opposed to the gods and goddesses of Shintoism, calmed down their opposition into a more conciliatory attitude. The theoretical basis for such a rapprochement was provided not by the triple-sūtras of Pure Realm Buddhism but by the Tendai doctrine based upon the Lotus Sūtra.

The Japanese native gods, exalted as they are from natural religious deities, kept their own distinctive existences intact. In this respect they differ completely from the Occidental counterpart, such as the ancient German religion, a trace of which is maintained in the form of the Christmas festivities within Christianity. The Japanese never considered it necessary to repudiate their religious faith in the native gods in order to become devoted followers of Buddhism. In this manner they brought about the conception of "God-Buddhas." It is generally seen even today that the ardent Buddhist is at the same time a pious worshipper of Shintoist gods. The majority of the Japanese pray before the shrines and at the same time pay homage to the temples, without being conscious of any contradiction. We may say that such a tendency has some merits on the one hand and demerits on the other. Critical comments will be given on other occasions. Anyhow, it is seen beginning with the reception of Buddhism in Japan.

Perhaps social scientists will in the end furnish us with statistical proof for my suggestion that the Japanese are a tolerant race. My own impression comes, as I have shown, from the study of documents and from personal observations.

1 F. S. C. NORTHROP, *The Taming of Nations,* 1952, Macmillan, p. 5.

2 These features were discussed in the author's work: *Tōyōjin no Shii Hōhō* (The Ways of Thinking of Eastern Peoples), vol. 1, Tokyo, 1948. A new edition is to be published by Shunjusha (Tokyo).

3 The author treated the naturalistic view of life in an essay: "Some Features of the Japanese Way of Thinking" (in *Monumenta Nipponica;* vol. XIV, Nos. 3–4, Tokyo, 1958–59, pp. 31–72).

4 *The Analects of Confucius,* 1, 12: 'In practicing the rules of propriety, a natural ease is to be prized." Here "a natural ease" is the translation of the Chinese word *wa. (Confucian Analects. Dr. Legge's Version.* Edited with notes by OGAERI Yoshio, Tokyo; Bunki Shoten, 1950, p. 4).

5 In the Chinese versions of Buddhist scriptures such words as *wakei (wakyō)* or *wagō* are frequently used.

6 The details are mentioned in the author's work: *Jihi* (Compassion), Kyoto, Heirakuji-Shoten, 1956, pp. 258–271.

7 *Shūgi-washo,* vol. 10, p. 1a (an old printed text, presumably to be found in the libraries of the University of Tokyo.)

8 See, for example, the stories of MIE-NO Uneme and the Emperors Kensō and Keitai; *Kojiki* (Records of Ancient Matters), translated by Basil Hall CHAMBERLAIN, supplement to vol. X, Translations of the Asiatic Society of Japan, Tokyo, 1906, pp. 402, 419, 424.

9 Ibid., pp. 213, 215.

10 *Pillar Edict* III (D. R. BHANDARKAR: *Asoka,* 3rd ed., University of Calcutta, 1955, p. 302.)

11 Op. cit. pp. 61–62.

12 Ibid., p. 62.

13 Ibid., pp. 4–5.

14 *Yerragudi Edict.*

15 Op. cit., p. 133.

16 Ibid., p. 64.

17 Ibid., pp. 215–216.

18 *Separate Kalinga Edicts,* II. (D. R. BHANDARKAR, op. cit., p. 329.)

19 *Pillar Edict* V (D. R. BHANDARKAR, op. cit., p. 270.)

20 *Dhammapada,* v. 163. (The Dhammapada with introductory essays, Pali text, English

translation and notes by S. RADHAKRISHNAN. Oxford University Press, London, 2nd impression, 1954, p. 113.)

21 Prince Shōtoku's *Shōmangyō-gisho*, ed. by HANAYAMA Shinshō, Iwanami, Tokyo, 1948, p. 34.

22 *Rock Edicts*, XIII.

23 Op. cit., p. 117.

24 Ibid., p. 137.

25 In the introductory manifesto of *Jinnō Shōtō-ki*, p. 585.

26 *Kanke Bunsō*, vol. 3 (*Kitano Bunsho*, vol. 2, p. 24; in *Kitano-shi*).

27 Cf. *Komo Toki*, vol. 1 (in *Yoshida Shōin Zenshū*, vol. 2, p. 263), ed. by Yamaguchi-ken-Kyoikukai, Iwanami, Tokyo, 1934.

28 *Jinnō-shōtōki*, Kōchū Nippon Bungaku Taikei, vol. 18.

29 *Shutsujō-shōgo*. Ed. and pub. by Kokumin Tosho Kabushiki Kaisha, Tokyo, 1925, p. 592.

30 Indians will be Indians; Chinese will be Chinese. We do not look down upon them or criticize them for being what they are.

31 According to legend, when Shinran paid a visit to the mausoleum of Prince Shōtoku at the age of nineteen, the Prince appeared in his dream and conferred upon him a verse in which is the phrase: "Japan is the country where Mahāyāna Buddhism is practiced." (GOTEN Ryōkū: *Takada Shinran Shōnin Seitōden*, vol. 1, in *Shinshū Zensho Shiden-bu*, p. 337. Cf. Hōkū: *Jōgū Taishi Shūiki*, in *Dainihon Bukkyō Zensho*, vol. 112, p. 142).

32 MIYAMOTO Shōson: *Chūdō-shisō oyobi sono Hattatsu*, Kyoto, Hozokan, 1944, pp. 888, 889.

33 HANAYAMA Shinsho: *Hokke Gisho no Kenkyū*, Tokyo, Oriental Library, 1933, p. 469.

34 *Yuimakyō Gisho*, in *Dainihon Bukkyō Zensho*, p. 141.

35 *Hokke Gisho, Nihon Bukkyō Zenshō*, p. 46.

36 Ibid., p. 28a. Similar expressions are found here and there. Cf. ibid., pp. 5a, 28a; 34a, and HANAYAMA: *Hokke Gisho no Kenkyū*, pp. 469, 489.

37 The phrase 得一切衆生殊勝供養 was interpreted "to make (Buddhas and Bodhisattvas) worship all living beings of distinction." It is needless to say that this is a twisted interpretation. An altruistic idea is introduced here. (Cf. HANAYAMA: *Shomangyo Gisho no Kenkyū*, pp. 434–437.)

38 HANAYAMA: *Hokke Gisho no Kenkyū*, pp. 386–7.

39. The famous story of abandonment of Prince Vessantara (*Jataka* No. 547), for example, is a good illustration.

40 HANAYAMA Shinshō: *Shōmangyō Gisho no Kenkyū*, p. 432.

41 This sentence is very famous and highly esteemed among Japanese. The original Sanskrit text runs as follows: "And the sermon he preaches will not fade from his memory. The popular maxims of common life, whether sayings or counsels, he will know how to reconcile with the rules of the low." *The Saddharmapundarika* or the *Lotus of the True Law*, translated by H. KERN, Oxford, 1909. See vol. 21, p. 351. Cf. also the edition by H. KERN and B. NANJIO, St.-Petersbourg, Imprimerie de l'Academie Imperiale des Sciences, 1912. Bibliotheca Buddhica 10, p. 372; and the edition by WOGIHARA Unrai and TSUCHIDA C., Tokyo, Seigo-kenkyūkai, 1934, p. 315. Here we find no mention of the words "politics" or "economics."

42 Chosui's *Commentary on the Sūragama-sūtra*, vol. 1a.

43 *Jōgai Ofumi* (帖外御文 Extra-canonical Letters), No. 52.

44 A Bodhisattva is a future Buddha who wants to save all living beings.

45 Founder of Chinese Zen Buddhism.

46 "Being destined for enlightenment," i.e. a candidate for enlightenment, in order to bring salvation to all mankind.

So far I have pointed out some important problems and salient features of Japanese philosophical thought. I hope the readers have come to notice that in the long history of Japanese thought nearly the same philosophical problems were discussed as in other traditions of the world even before the over-all introduction of Western civilization, but in a different setting.

However, I regret that my explanation has not been clear enough to solve these philosophical problems and to evaluate them as should have been done in such a way as is worth while, because my stock of knowledge is limited and the space assigned by the Kokusai Bunka Shinkokai is also limited. I must admit that many works by ancient Japanese should be investigated, and that they have been unfortunately been neglected by Japanese intellectuals. This fact might strike foreigners as strange, but there have been some reasons.

After the Meiji Restoration it was encouraged by the authorities to cut off our own religious tradition to replace it with nationalism and Emperor worship which were exceedingly forced till the end of World War II. Intellectuals have paid attention to the West alone. Western, chiefly German, philosophy alone was taught among philosophers. Whenever a philosophical work is published in German or in French, it is immediately translated into Japanese. It is said jokingly, therefore, that philosophical books written in German sell more in Japan than in Germany itself. There has been no Japanese philosopher who claims to specialize in Japanese thought.

It is true that Japanese tradition was exceedingly esteemed in the past, but it was done by ultranationalists, generals and high officials, and not by intellectuals. The latter have been mostly antagonistic to the movements of the former, although not successfully. The studies carried on by some nationalist scholars were forced, twisted and not convincing.

In Japanese national universities there is no chair for Japanese philosophy. Those chairs established for it before the war were abolished, and any project to newly establish one is met by strong opposition on the part of professors who are very watchful of the movement to recover nationalist influence. But I think Japanese philosophy in the past should be examined apart from nationalistic interest.

In Japan Buddhist studies are now flourishing, but most scholars are engaged in philological approaches to them and not in philosophical ones. Works by medieval Buddhist theologians are new resources to be exploited. They contain a lot of absurd explanations when we check them closely with their Sanskrit originals, and so capable scholars are looking down upon them with contempt. They may represent, say, seventy percent absurd and arbitrary sayings, but the remaining thirty percent will exhibit us sayings of philosophical value, just as medieval theological works by Christian, Islamic and Hindu theologians will do. It is a pity that only sectarian-minded theologians of the present time read them and scholars of modern approach do not read them. These works will assure us with great amount of philosophical insight. Things are more or less the same with Shinto and Confucian studies in Japan. Their ways of explaining things are highly twisted and far-fetched, but in most of the cases we can find the necessity for that because they are urged by the need of philosophical consistency and the sociological needs of the day.

Japanese Buddhist logicians have left a huge amount of logical works which are commentaries on Chinese-translated Indian treatises. I do not know how to deal with them adequately; few modern studies have been made in this field. These treasures are left to future investigations by rising scholars.

A BIBLIOGRAPHY OF WORKS ON JAPANESE THOUGHT IN WESTERN LANGUAGES

Abbreviations
CIIB Press: Cultural Interchange Institute for Buddhists,
c/o Hong-wanji-Temple, Tsukiji, Chuo-ku, Tokyo, Japan
HJAS: Harvard Journal of Asiatic Studies, Cambridge,
Massachusetts
TASJ; Transactions of Asiatic Society of Japan, Yokohama
and Tokyo.

I General Works

As regards the books on purely philosophical thought of pre-Meiji period not many works exist. But among works on religion, ethics and aesthetics, there are some references or clues to philosophical thinking of Japan.

Gino K. PIOVESANA. *Recent Japanese Philosophical Thought 1862– 1962. A Survey.* Tokyo, Enderle Bookstore, 1963. Reviewed by M. SCALIGERO, *Philosophy East and West* vol. 15, 1965, pp. 381–383.

Japanese Religion and Philosophy: A Guide to Japanese Reference and Research Materials. Compiled by Donald Holzman, with MOTOYAMA Yukihiko and others. Edited by J. K. YAMAGIWA. Ann ARBOR, the University of Michigan, Center for Japanese Studies, Bibliographical Series, No. 7, 1959. This is an introduction to works written in Japanese.

II Japanese Culture

Wm. Theodore DEBARY, Donald KEENE and TSUNODA Ryusaku. *Sources of the Japanese Tradition.* New York, Columbia University Press, 1958.

Japan in the Chinese Dynastic Histories. Translated by TSUNODA R. Calif., South Pasadena, Calif., P. D. and I. PERKINS, 1951.

TSUCHIHASHI P. Yachita. *Japanese Chronological Tables.* Tokyo, Sophia University, 1952.

Japan: Its Lands, People and Culture. Compiled by The Japanese National Commission for UNESCO, 1959.

Translations from Early Japanese Literature. By Edwin O. REISCHAUER and Joseph K. YAMAGIWA. Harvard University Press, 1951.

Religions in Japan at Present. The Institute for Research in Religious Problems.

Proceedings of the IXth International Congress for the History of Religions, 1958. Tokyo, Maruzen, 1960.

Religious Studies in Japan. Edited by Japanese Association for Religious Studies and Japanese Organizing Committee of the Ninth International Congress for the History of Religions. Tokyo, Maruzen, 1959.

Transactions of the International Conference of Orientalists in Japan.
No. I–V, 1956–1960. Tokyo, Toho Gakkai (Institute of Eastern
Culture).

III Japanese Religion in General

ANESAKI Masaharu. *History of Japanese Religion.* London, Kegan
Paul, Trench, Trubner, 1930. Reprinted by Tuttle Company.

ANESAKI Masaharu. *Religious Life of the Japanese People.* Revised by
KISHIMOTO Hideo. Tokyo, Kokusai Bunka Shinkokai, 1961.
Agency: East-West Center Press, Honolulu.

Wilhelm GUNDERT. *Japanische Religionsgeschichte: Die Religionen
der Japaner und Koreaner in geschichtlichem Abriss dargestellt.* Tokyo-
Stuttgart, 1935. Reviewed by H. DUMOULIN, *Monumenta Nipponica,* vol. 1, 1938, pp. 282–283.

Heinrich DUMOULIN. *Östliche Meditation und christliche Mystik.*
Freiburg/München, Verlag Karl Alber, 1966.

IV Japanese Buddhism

a) General Outline

(Recent Works)

E. Dale SAUNDERS. *Buddhism in Japan, with an Outline of Its
Origins in India.* Philadelphia, University of Pennsylvania
Press, 1964.

HANAYAMA Shinsho. *A History of Japanese Buddhism.* Tr. by
YAMAMOTO Kosho. Tokyo, the CIIB Press, 1960.

ISHII Mamine Shimpo. *Japanese Buddhism.* Tokyo, Zojoji Press,
1959.

WATANABE Shoko. *Japanese Buddhism: a Critical Appraisal.*
Tokyo, Kokusai Bunka Shinkokai, 1964.

Kenneth W. MORGAN. The Path of the Buddha. New York,
Ronald Press, 1956, pp. 307–400.

(Earlier Works)

Sir Charles ELIOT. *Japanese Buddhism.* London, Edward Arnold
& Co., 1935. The most detailed outline in English even in
the present.

SUZUKI D. T. *Japanese Buddhism.* Tokyo, Board of Tourist

Industry, Japanese Government Railways, 1938.

J. B. PRATT. *The Pilgrimage of Buddhism. and a Buddhist Pilgrimage* New York, Macmillan, 1925, pp. 436–671.

A. K. REISCHAUER. *Studies in Japanese Buddhism.* New York, Macmillan, 1925.

Robert Cornell ARMSTRONG. *Buddhism and Buddhists in Japan.* New York, 1927.

ANESAKI Masaharu. *Quelques pages de l'histoire religieuse du Japon:* conferences faites au College de France. Paris, 1921.

ANESAKI Masaharu. *Katam Karaniyam:* Lectures, Essays and Studies. Tokyo, Herald Press, 1934.

Otto ROSENBERG. *Die Weltanschaung des modernen Buddhismus im fernen Osten.* Heidelberg, O. Harrassowitz, 1924.

TAKAKUSU Junjiro. *The Essentials of Buddhist Philosophy.* Honolulu, The University of Hawaii Press, 1947. A reliable work as an introduction to Japanese Buddhism, although this may not be so easy for foreign readers to read.

Marimum Willem de VISSER. *Ancient Buddhism in Japan: Sūtras and Ceremonies in Use in the Seventh and Eighth Centuries A.D. and Their History in Later Times.* 3 vols. Leiden, 1935.

SUZUKI D. T. *Buddhist Philosophy and Its Effects on the Life and Thought of the Japanese People.* Tokyo, Kokusai Bunka Shinkokai (The Society for International Cultural Relations), 1936.

Rev. James SUMMERS. Buddhism, and Traditions Concerning Its Introduction into Japan TASJ. Tokyo, 1907.

Arthur LLOYD. Formative Elements of Japanese Buddhism. TASJ. Tokyo, 1908.

Arthur LLOYD. *The Creed of Half Japan: Historical Sketches of Japanese Buddhism.* London, 1911.

Dwight GODDARD. *Buddha, Truth, and Brotherhood: an Epitome of Many Buddhist Scriptures.* Translated from the Japanese. American ed. Santa Barbara, California, 1934.

b) Buddhism and Japanese

NAKAMURA Hajime. *Ways of Thinking of Eastern Peoples: India-China-Tibet-Japan.* Edited by Philip P. WIENER. Honolulu, East-West Center, 1964. pp. 343–587.

NAKAMURA Hajime. *The Ways of Thinking of Eastern Peoples.* Published by the Japanese National Commission for UNESCO. Tokyo, 1960. (out of print)

TAMURA Y. *Living Buddhism in Japan.* Tokyo, International Institute for the Study of Religions, 1961.

Japan and Buddhism. The Association of the Buddhajayanti, Tokyo, 1959.

NAKARAI, WADA Toyozo. *A Study of the Impact of Buddhism upon Japanese Life as Revealed in the Odes of the Kokin-shū.* Greenfield, Indiana, 1931.

Georges BONNEAU. *La sensibilite japonaise.* 3 ed. Tokyo, 1934.

Kogoshui, Gleanings from Ancient Stories. Tr. by KATO Genchi and HOSHINO Hikoshiro. 4th ed. Tokyo, Meiji Japan Society, 1937.

HANAYAMA Shinsho. *The Way of Deliverance: Three Years with the Condemned Japanese War Criminals.* New York, Charles Scribner's Sons, 1950.

YAMAMOTO Kosho. *The Udumbara: Tales from Buddhist Japan.* Tokyo, the CIIB, Tsukiji-Hongwanji, 1959.

Courses on Religion in Universities. Tokyo, The International Institute for the Study of Religions, Incorporated.

ASAKAWA K. *Social Reactions of Buddhism in Medieval Japan.* (In Panama-Pacific Historical Congress, 1915. The Pacific Ocean in History—ed. by Morse STEPHANS and Herbert E. BOLTON. New York, 1917.)

J. M. JAMES. *Descriptive Notes on the Rosaries (Jiu-Dzu) as used by the Different Sects of Buddhists in Japan.* TASJ. Tokyo, 1905.

ANESAKI Masaharu. *Buddhist Art in Its Relation to Buddhist Ideals, with Special Reference to Buddhism in Japan.* Boston and New York, 1915.

ICHIKAWA Sanki (ed.) *Japanese Noh Dramas,* 3 vols. Tokyo, The

Nippon Gakujutsu Shinkokai.

c) Prince Shotoku

ANESAKI Masaharu. *Prince Shotoku, The Sage-Statesman and His Mahasattva Ideal.* Tokyo, The Boonjudo Publishing House, 1948.

ANESAKI Masaharu. *Prince Shotoku, The Sage-Statesman of Japan.* Nara, Horyuji Temple.

Friedrich HEILER and NAKAMURA H. *My Impression in front of the Mausoleum of Prince Shōtoku.* Osaka, Eifukuji Temple, 1961.

MOCHIZUKI Kazunori. *The Mausoleum of Prince Shotoku.* Osaka, Eifukuji Temple, 1958.

MOCHIZUKI Kazunori. *A Treatise on Prince Shotoku.* Tokyo, New Educational Research Institute, 1959.

ANESAKI Masaharu. The Foundation of Buddhist Culture in Japan. The Buddhist Ideals as Conceived and Carried Out by the Prince-Regent Shotoku. *Monumenta Nipponica,* vol. 6, 1943, Nos. 1–2, pp. 1–12.

BOHNER Herman. *Shōtoku Taishi.* Tokyo, Deutsche Gesellschaft für Natur- und Völker Kunde Ostasiens, 1940.

This is a voluminous book in German amounting to 1003 pages. Reviewed by C. von WEEGMANN, *Monumenta Nipponica,* vol. 5, 1942, pt. 2, pp. 279–285.

d) Sanron Sect

Richard A. GARD. "Why did the Mādhyamika decline?" *Journal of Indian and Buddhist Studies,* vol. 5, No. 2, March 1957, pp. 619–623.

e) The Kegon Sect

Serge ELISSEEFF. The Bommokyo and the Great Buddha of the Todaiji. (HJAS. Vol. I, 1936, pp. 84–96)

f) Tendai Philosophy

UI Hakuju. A Study of Japanese Tendai Buddhism. *Philosophical Studies of Japan,* published by Japan Society for the Promotion of Science, Tokyo, vol. I, 1959, pp. 33–74.

g) Shingon Sect

Kobo Daishi. *(The Mikkyo Bunka: The Quarterly Reports on the Esoteric Buddhism.)* 1949–1957. Koyasan University.

TAJIMA Ryujun. *Les deux grands Mandalas et la doctrine de l'eso-terisme Shingon.* Tokyo, Comite de publication de l'ouvre posthume du Rev. TAJIMA, 1959.

Hermann BOHNER. Kobo Daishi. *Monumenta Nipponica,* vol. 6, 1943, Nos. 1–2, pp. 266–313. In this article the writer examines various biographies of Kobo Daishi (in German).

Helmuth von GLASENAPP. Die Stellung der esoterischen Sekten Japans in der Geschichte der buddhistischen Überlieferuug. *Ostasiatische Studien,* Berlin, Akademie-Verlag, 1959, S. 81–84.

Sangō Shīki (三教指歸)

HAKEDA Y. S. *The Religious Novel of Kukai. Monumenta Nipponica,* vol. 20, Nos. 3–4, 1965, pp. 283–297.

Some important works by Kukai or Kobo Daishi were translated into English by the Translation Institute in Koyasan University:

1) *Sokushin Jōbutsugi* (即身成佛義 The Doctrine of Attaining Buddhahood While Living in Human Body). *The Mikkyō Bunka,* vol. 27, pp. 1–12; vol. 28, pp. 13–22; vols. 29–30, pp. 23–32; vol. 31, pp. 1–12; vol. 32, pp. 1–10; vol. 33, pp. 1–14; vol. 34, pp. 1–10; vol. 38, pp. 1–19, 1954–1956.

2) *Unjigi* (吽字義 The Doctrine of the Syllable Hūṃ). *The Mikkyō Bunka,* vol. 17, pp. 1–10; vol. 18, pp. 11–20; vol. 19, pp. 21–32; vol. 20, pp. 33–42; vol. 21, pp. 43–54; vol. 22, pp. 55–62; vol. 23, pp. 63–72; vols. 24–25, pp. 73–82, 1951–1953.

3) *Shōji Jissōgi* (聲字實相義 A Treatise on the Meaning of Voice and Syllable and Reality). *The Mikkyō Bunka,* vol. 7, pp. 1–10; vol. 8, pp. 1–10; vols. 9–10, pp. 1–12; vol. 11, pp. 1–12; vol. 12, pp. 1–12; vol. 13, pp. 1–12, 1948–1950.

h) Pure Realm Buddhism

YAMAMOTO Kosho. *An Introduction to Shin Buddhism.* Ube, Yamaguchi-ken, Karinbunko, 1963. This is a detailed and comprehensive introduction.

H. COATES and ISHIZUKA. *Honen, the Buddhist Saint, His Life and Teaching.* 6 vols. Kyoto, the Society for the Publication of Sacred Books of the World, 1949.

Paul CARUS. *Amitabha; A Story of Buddhist Theology.* Chicago, Open Court, 1906.

FUJIMOTO R. *An Outline of the Triple Sūtra of Shin Buddhism,* vol. I, 1955. Kyoto, Honpa Hongwanji Press.

UTSUKI Nishu. *The Shin Sect, a School of Mahayana Buddhism, Its Teaching, Brief History, and Present-day Conditions.* Publication Bureau of Buddhist Books, Honpa Hongwanji, Kyoto, Japan, 1937.

Selections from the Nippon Seishin (Japanese Spirit) Library. Edited by AKEGARASU Haya. Kososha, Kitayasuda, Ishikawa-ken, Japan, 1936.

James TROUP. *On the Tenets of the Shinshu or 'True Sect' of Buddhists. TASJ.* 1907.

Rev. NAKAI Gendo. *Shinran and His Religion of Pure Faith.* Kyoto, The Shinshu Research Institute, 1937.

Guide Book to the Buildings of the West Hongwanji. Kyoto, West Hongwanji.

(Texts)

The Kyogyoshinsho or the 'Teaching, Practice, Faith, and Attainment.' Translated by YAMAMOTO Kosho. Tokyo, Karinbunko, 1958.

The Shinshu Seiten. The Holy Scripture of Shinshu. Honolulu, The Honpa Hongwanji Mission of Hawaii, 1955. The scriptures other than the *Kyogyoshinsho* are translated.

UTSUKI Nishu. *Selected Texts of Shin Buddhism.*

YAMAMOTO Kosho. *The Private Letters of Shinran Shonin.* Tokyo, Okazakiya, 1946.

Tannisho. A Tract Deploring Heresies of Faith. Kyoto, Higashi Hongwanji Shamusho, 1961.

Shinran-shonin's Tannisho with Buddhist Psalms. Tr. by INAGAKI Saizo. Eishinsha, 510, Nishikubo Takagi, Nishinomiya City,

1949.

KANAMATSU Kenryo. *Naturalness*. Los Angeles, The White Path Society, 1956.

MIKOGAMI Eryu. "Outline of the Notes Lamenting Differences." Published in *Journal of Ryukoku University*. Kyoto, 1953.

IMADATE Tosui. *The Tannishō (Tracts on Deploring the Heterodoxies)*. Kyoto, 1928.

i) The Nichiren Sect

ANESAKI Masaharu. *The Buddhist Prophet*. Harvard, 1916.

SATOMI Kishio. *Japanese Civilization, Its Significance and Realization. Nichirenism and the Japanese National Principles*. London, 1923.

Nichiren's *The True Object of Worship*. Tr. by MURANO Senchu. The Young East Association, 1, 3-chome, Tsukiji, Chuo-ku, Tokyo, 1954.

j) Zen Buddhism

1) Outline

There are many works on Zen in English by Japanese authors, but they represent one branch or tendency or another, and cannot help but being one-sided. Strange to say, a rather objective, overall historical sketch was given by a German Catholic Father.

Heinrich DUMOULIN. *Zen. Geschichte und Gestalt*. Bern, Francke Verlag, 1959.

Heinrich DUMOULIN. *A History of Zen Buddhism*. New York, Pantheon Books, 1963.

2) Chinese Zen Buddhism in General and Rinzai Sect

John BLOFELD. *The Zen Teaching of Huang Po, on the Transmission of Mind*. An Evergreen Original, New York, the Grove Press, 1959.

SUZUKI Daisetz Teitaro. *Living by Zen*. The Sanseido Publishing Company, Kanda, Tokyo, 1949.

SUZUKI Daisetz Teitaro. *The Zen Doctrine of No-Mind*. London, 1949.

SUZUKI Daisetz Teitaro. *An Introduction to Zen Buddhism* (2nd ed., London, Rider and Co., 1957).

SUZUKI Daisetz Teitaro. *Essays in Zen Buddhism,* First Series (2nd ed., New York, Harper and Bros., 1949).

SUZUKI Daisetz Teitaro. *Essays in Zen Buddhism,* Second Series (2nd ed., London, Rider and Co., 1957).

SUZUKI Daisetz Teitaro. *Essays in Zen Buddhism,* Third Series (2nd ed., London, Rider and Co., 1953).

SUZUKI Daisetz Teitaro. *A Manual of Zen Buddhism* (2nd ed., London, Rider and Co., 1957).

SUZUKI Daisetz Teitaro. *The Training of the Zen Buddhist Monk.* (1st American ed., New York, University Books, 1959).

SUZUKI Daisetz Teitaro. Zen Buddhism. *Monumenta Nipponica,* vol. 1, 1938, pp. 48–57. He discusses the thought of Zen masters of China who were influential in Japan.

SUZUKI Daisetz Teitaro. *Zen and Japanese Buddhism.* Tokyo, Japan Travel Bureau, Charles E. Tuttle Co., 1958.

SUZUKI Daisetz Teitaro. *Zen Buddhism: Selected Writings of D. T. Suzuki.* Ed. by William BARRETT. (A Doubleday Anchor Book). New York, Doubleday, 1956.

SUZUKI Daisetz Teitaro. *The Ten Oxherding Pictures.* Sekai Seiten Kanko Kyokai, No. 496. Hanatate-cho, Kamigyo-ku XII, Kyoto, 1948.

SUZUKI Daisetz Teitaro. *Buddhist Symbolism, Published in Symbols and Values: An Initial Study.* Thirteenth Symposium of the Conference on Science, Philosophy and Religion. Ed. by L. BRYSON, L. FINKELSTEIN, R. M. MACIVER, and R. McKEON. Harper and Brothers. New York and London, 1954.

SUZUKI Daisetz Teitaro. *The Philosophy of Zen. Philosophy East and West.* Vol. I, No. 2, 1951.

SUZUKI Daisetz Teitaro. *Zen: A Reply to HuShih. Philosophy East and West.* Vol. III, No. 1, 1953.

Buddhism and Culture: Dedicated to Dr. SUZUKI Daisetz Teitaro in Commemoration of His Ninetieth Birthday. Edited by YAMAGUCHI Susumu. Kyoto, Suzuki Foundation, 1960.

R. H. BLYTH. *Zen in English Literature and Oriental Classics.* Tokyo, Hokuseido, 1948.

R. H. BLYTH. *Zen and Zen Classics,* vol. I. Tokyo, Hokuseido.

H. DUMOULIN and Ruth F. SASAKI. *The Development of Chinese Zen after the Sixth Patriarch in the Light of Mumonkan.* The First Zen Institute of America, New York, 1953.

Alan W. WATTS. *The Spirit of Zen.* (The Wisdom of the East Series.) London, 1936.

Alan W. WATTS. *Zen.* Stanford, California, 1948.

Alan W. WATTS. *The Way of Zen.* (A Mentor Book). New York, Pantheon Books, Inc., 1957.

Erich FROMM, SUZUKI Daisetz Teitaro, R. de MARTINO. *Zen Buddhism and Psycho-analysis.*

Ruth Fuller SASAKI. *Rinzai Zen Study for Foreigners in Japan.* Kyoto, the First Zen Institute of America in Japan. (107 Daitokuji-cho, Murasakino, Kyoto, 1960); The First Zen Institute of America, Inc., 156 Waverly Place, New York 14.

MIURA Isshû and Ruth Fuller SASAKI. *"The Zen Kôan."* Kyoto, The First Zen Institute of American in Japan, 1965. Reviewed by H. DUMOULIN, *Monumenta Nipponica,* vol. XXII, Nos. 1–2, 1967, pp. 220–222.

3) Soto Sect of Zen Buddhism

MASUNAGA Reiho. *The Soto Approach to Zen.* Tokyo, Layman Buddhist Society Press, 1956. This work includes translations of some chapters of *Shōbōgenzō.*

MASUNAGA Reiho. *Zen for Daily Living.* Tokyo, Shunjusha, 1964.

Heinrich DUMOULIN. "Die religiöse Metaphysik des japa-

nischen Zen-Meisters Dōgen," *Saeculum* XII, Heft 3, S. 205–236.
This is one of the rare works dealing with philosophy as such.

Zen. The Way to a Happy Life. Compiled and published by the Headquarters of the Soto Sect, Tokyo, n.d. In this work new methods such as measurement of waves in electroencephalographic studies are applied.

Ernest S. HUNT. Gleanings from Soto Zen, 1957. Honolulu, Soto Mission.

NUKARIYA Kaiten. *The Religion of the Samurai. A Study of Zen Philosophy and Discipline in China and Japan.* London, 1913.

Sokei-An (alias SASAKI Shigetsu). *Cat's Yawn.* New York, First Zen Institute of America, 1947.

FUJIMOTO Rindō. *The Way of Zazen.* Cambridge, Mass., Cambridge Buddhist Association, 1961.

Syōbōgenzō-Zuimonki. Wortgetreue Niederschrift der lehrreichen Worte Dōgen-Zenzis über den wahren Buddhismus. Ausgewählt, übersetzt und mit kurzer Biographie sowie einem Anhang versehen von IWAMOTO Hidemasa. Tokyo, Sankibo, 1943.

(Texts)

Dōgen's *"Fukan Zazengi"* (普勧坐禅儀 Teachings to Promote Meditation) was translated into German by H. DUMOULIN, *Monumenta Nipponica,* vol. 12, Nos. 3–4, 1956, pp. 183–190.

Shushōgi (修證義). "Prinzipien der Übung und Erleuchtung. Eine Zenschrift für Laien." Translated into German by ISHIMOTO K. and P. E. NABERFELD. *Monumenta Nipponica,* vol. 6, Nos. 1–2, pp. 355–369.

Keizan (1268–1325)'s *Zazen Yōjinki* (坐禅用心記) was translated into German by Heinrich DUMOULIN, *Monumenta Nipponica,* vol. 13, Nos. 3–4, 1957, pp. 147–167.

Then in his *Östliche Meditation und christliche Mystik*. Freiburg/München, Verlag Karl Alber, 1966, S. 291–307.

4) Obaku Sect of Zen Buddhism

SHIBATA Masumi. *Le Sermon de Tetsugen sur le Zen*. Tokyo, Risosha, 1960.

5) Contemporary Zen

UEDA Daisuke. *Zen and Science*. A Treatise on Causality and Freedom. Tokyo, Risosha, 1963. This is a treatise from the standpoint of a scientist.

Betty and Van Meter AMES. *Japan and Zen*. Cincinnati, University of Cincinnati, 1961. Prof. V. M. AMES is an American professor of philosophy.

Ingeborg Y. WENDT. *Zen, Japan und der Westen*. München, Paul List Verlag, 1961.

Philip KAPLEAU. *The Three Pillars of Zen. Teaching/Practice/ Enlightenment*. Tokyo, John Weatherhill, 1965.

H. DUMOULIN. Die Zen-Erleuchtung in neueren Erlebnisberichten, *Numen,* vol. 10, Fasc. 2, Aug. 1963. In this article present-day Zen is discussed.

H. DUMOULIN. Technique and Personal Devotion in the Zen Exercise. *Studies in Japanese Culture*. Tokyo, Sophia University, 1963, pp. 17–40.

k) Buddhist Thinkers of the Modern or Tokugawa Period

Hakuin's "Yasen Kanna" (夜船閑話 A Chat on a Boat in the Evening), translated by R. D. M. SHAW and Wilhelm SCHIFFER, *Monumenta Nipponica,* vol. 13, Nos. 1–2, 1957, pp. 101–127.

YANAGI Muneyoshi. "Mokujiki Gogyō Shōnin. Bonze und Bildschnitzer der Edozeit." *Monumenta Nipponica,* vol. 6, Nos. 1–2, 1943, pp. 202–218.

1) Bibliography

BANDO S., HANAYAMA S., SATO R., SAYEKI S., and SHIMA K. *A Bibliography on Japanese Buddhism*. Tokyo, CIIB Press, 1958.

HANAYAMA Shinsho. *A Bibliography of Buddhism*. Tokyo, Hokuseido (in press).

V Shintoism

  a) Outline

KATO Genchi. *A Study of Shinto, The Religion of the Japanese Nation*. Tokyo, The Zaidan-Hojin-Meiji-Seitoku-Kinen-Gakkai (Meiji Japan Society), 1926. A very scholarly work, fully documented. Still worth while.

An Outline of Shinto Teachings. Compiled by Shinto Committee for the IXth International Congress for the History of Religions. Tokyo, 1958.

Shinto Shrines and Festivals. Tokyo, Kokugakuin University, 1958.

Guide Book of Shinto Shrines. Tokyo, Kokugakuin University, 1958.

Basic Terms of Shinto. Tokyo, Kokugakuin University, 1958.

KONO Shozo. "Kannagara no Michi (神ながらの道)" (in Engl.). *Monumenta Nipponica*, vol. 3, No. 2, 1940, pp. 9–31.

D. C. HOLTOM. "The Meaning of Kami." *Monumenta Nipponica*, vol. 3, 1940, p. 1 ff.; 392 ff.; vol. 4, 1941, pt. 2, pp. 25–68.

KATŌ Genchi's two books in Japanese are very valuable. They were fure fully appreciated by Heinrich DUMOULIN, *Monumenta Nipponica*, vol. 1, pt. 2, 1938, pp. 284–292 (in German).

  b) Mediaeval Shintoism

Jinnō Shōtōki, Buch von der Wahren Gott-Kaiser-Herrshafts-Linie, verfasst von KITABATAKE Chikafusa. Übersetzt, eingeleitet und erläutert von Hermann BOHNER. Tokyo, Japanisch-Deutsches Kulturinstitut, 1938. Reviewed by J. B. KRAUS, *Monumenta Nipponica*, vol. 1, 1938, pp. 285–286; by H. ZACHERT, *Monumenta Nipponica*, vol. 3, 1940, No. 2, pp. 311–312.

Saka's Diary of a Pilgrim to Ise. Translated by A. L. SADLER with an introduction by KATŌ Genchi. Edited by the Meiji Japan Society, Tokyo, 1940. Reviewed by R. H. VAN GULLIK, *Monumenta Nipponica*, vol. 4, 1941, pt. 2, pp. 297–298.

Yuiitsu-Shintō Myōbō-yōshū (唯一神道名法要集), probably written by YOSHIDA Kanetomo (吉田兼倶 1435–1511), was translated into German by ISHIBASHI T. and H. DUMOULIN, *Monumenta Nipponica,* vol. 3, 1940, No. 1, pp. 182–239.

KATŌ Genchi. "The Theological System of Urabe no Kaneto-mo." *Transactions and Proceedings of the Japan Society,* London, vol. 28.

c) Shintoism in the Modern or Tokugawa Period

MURAOKA Tsunetsugu. *Studies in Shinto Thought.* Translated by D. M. BROWN and James T. ARAKI. Tokyo, Japanese National Commission for UNESCO, 1964. Reviewed by Francisco Pérez RUIZ. *Monumenta Nipponica,* vol. 21, Nos. 1–2, 1966, pp. 212–214.

Heinrich DUMOULIN, H. STOLTE und W. SCHIFFER. "Die Entwicklung der Kokugaku dargestellt in ihren Haupt-vertretern," *Monumenta Nipponica,* vol. 2, 1939, pp. 140–164.

KADA Azumamaro (1669–1736)'s *Sō-Gakkō-kei* (創學校啓 Gesuch um die Errichtung einer Kokugaku-Schule) was translated into German by H. DUMOULIN, *Monumenta Nipponica,* vol. 3, No. 2, 1940, pp. 230–249.

Two texts by KAMO Mabuchi (1697–1769), *Uta no Kokoro no Uchi* and *Niimanabi* (爾比末奈妣) were translated into German by H. DUMOULIN, *Monumenta Nipponica,* vol. 4, 1941, pt. 1, pp. 192–206; pt. 2, pp. 240–258. They are treatises on Japanese poetry.

KAMO Mabuchi's *Kokuikō* (国意考) was translated into German by H. DUMOULIN, *Monumenta Nipponica,* vol. 2, 1939, pp. 165–192.

KAMO Mabuchi's *Commentary on the Norito of the Toshigoi-no-Matsuri* (祈年祭)" was translated into German by H. DUMOULIN, *Monumenta Nipponica,* vol. 12, Nos. 1–2, 1956, pp. 121–156. Nos. 3–4, pp. 101–130.

The Innovation of the Way of Poetry by KAMO Mabuchi was

discussed by H. DUMOULIN, *Monumenta Nipponica,* vol. 6, 1943, Nos. 1–2, pp. 110–145.

H. DUMOULIN. *Kamo Mabuchi.* Tokyo, Sophia University, 1943.

MOTOORI Norinaga's *Naobi no Mitama* (直毘靈) was translated into German by Hans STOLTE, *Monumenta Nipponica,* vol. 2, 1939, pp. 193–211.

HIRATA Atsutane's *Taidō Wakumon* (大道或問) was translated into German by Wilhelm SCHIFFER, *Monumenta Nipponica,* vol. 2, 1939, pp. 212–236.

d) Sectarian Shintoism before the Meiji Restoration

Charles William HEPNER. *The Kurozumi Sect of Shinto* Tokyo, Meiji Japan Society, 1935. Reviewed by H. DUMOULIN, *Monumenta Nipponica,* vol. 2, No. 2, 1939, pp. 322–324.

Delwin B. SCHNEIDER. *Konkōkyō.* A Japanese Religion. Tokyo, International Institute for the Study of Religions, 1962.

VI Confucianism

Confucianism in Action. Ed. by Arthur F. WRIGHT and David S. VIVISON. Stanford University Press, 1959.

KITAMURA Sawakichi. *Grundriss der Ju-Lehre.* Tokyo, Maruzen, 1935. Reviewed by W. SCHIFFER, *Monumenta Nipponica,* vol. 2, 1939, pp. 320–322.

J. R. McEWAN. *The Political Writings of Ogyū Sorai.* Cambridge, Cambridge University Press, 1962. Reviewed by Joseph PITTAU, *Monumenta Nipponica,* vol. 17, 1962, p. 341.

Onna Daigaku (女大學). (Ein Frauenspiegel der Tokugawa-zeit.) translated into German by KOIKE Kenji, *Monumenta Nipponica,* vol. 2, No. 2, 1939, pp. 254–263.

Horst HAMMITZSCH. Die Mito-Schule und ihre programmatischen Schriften *Bairi Sensei Hiin, Kōdōkanki, Kōdōkangakusoku, Seiki no Uta* in Üebersetzung. Ein Beitrag zur Geistesgeschichte der Tokugawa-Zeit. Tokyo, Deutsche Gesellschaft für Natur- und Völkerkunde Ostasiens, 1939. Reviewed by H. DUMOULIN, *Monumenta Nipponica,* vol. 3, No. 2, 1940, pp. 327–329.

Horst HAMMITZSCH. "Aizawa Seishisai (1782–1863) und sein Werk Shinron." *Monumenta Nipponica,* vol. 3, No. 1, 1940, pp. 61–74.

VII Shingaku School
The outline of Shingaku is set forth in the following article:—
Horst HAMMITZSCH. Shingaku. Eine Bewegung der Volksauf-klärung und Volkserziehung in der Tokugawazeit. *Monumenta Nipponica,* vol. 4, 1941, Pt. 1, pp. 1–32.

VIII Japanese Christianity
Christianity in Japan. *A Bibliography of Japanese aud Chinese Sources.* Pt. 1 (1543–1858). Tokyo, International Christian University, 1960.

Hubert CIESLIK. Kirishitan-Literatur der Nachkriegszeit. *Monumenta Nipponica,* vol. 16, Nos. 3–4, 1960–61, pp. 187–213.

Charles W. IGLEHART. *A Century of Protestant Christianity in Japan.* Tokyo, Charles E. Tuttle Co., 1960.

MASUTANI Fumio. *A Comparative Study of Buddhism and Christianity.* Tokyo, CIIB Press ,1959.

T. N. CALLAWAY. *Japanese Buddhism and Christianity.* Tokyo, Shinkyo Shuppansha, 1957.

Pierre HUMBERTCLAUDE. *Myōtei Mondō* 妙貞問答: Une apologétique chrétienne japonaise de 1605. *Monumenta Nipponica,* vol. 1, Pt. 2. 1938, pp. 223–256; vol. 2, 1939, pp. 237–267.

HAYASHI Razan's *Hai-Yaso* (排耶蘇 Anti-Jesus) was translated into German by Hans MÜLLER, *Monumenta Nipponica,* vol. 2, No. 1, 1939, pp. 268–275.

IX Mediaeval Thought
HIRAIZUMI H. "Der Einfluss der Mappō-Lehre in der japanischen Geschichte." *Monumenta Nipponica,* vol. 1, 1938, pp. 58–69.

The *Honchō-Shinsen-Den* (本朝神仙傳). was translated into German by Hermann BOHNER, *Monumenta Nipponica,* vol. 13, Nos. 1–2, pp. 129–152.

X The Thought of the Modern or Tokugawa Period
Robert N. BELLAH. *Tokugawa Religion. The Values of Pre-Indus-trial Japan.* Glencoe, Illinois, The Free Press, 1957. Reviewed by

P. Beonio-Brocchieri, *Monumenta Nipponica,* vol. 12, Nos. 1–2, 1956, pp. 226–227.

Horst Hammitzsch. "Kangaku und Kokugaku. Ein Beitrag zur Geistesgeschichte der Tokugawazeit." *Monumenta Nipponica,* vol. 2, 1939, pp. 1–23.

Paolo Benio-Brochieri. *Religiosita e Ideologia alle Origini del Giappone Moderno.* Milano, Istituto per Gli Studi di Politica Internazionale, 1965.

Nakamura Hajime. Suzuki Shosan (1579–1655) and the Spirit of Capitalism in Japanese Buddhism. *Monumenta Nipponica,* vol. XXII, Nos. 1–2 1967, pp. 1–14.

XI Independent Thinkers

Gino K. Piovesana. A Bibliographical Note on Miura Baien. *Monumenta Nipponica,* vol. 19, Nos. 3–4, 1964, pp. 232–234.

Kato Shuichi. Tominaga Nakamoto, (1715–46), A Tokugawa Iconoclast. *Monumenta Nipponica,* vol. XXII, Nos. 1–2, 1967, pp. 177–210.

Other articles on independent thinkers are mentioned in the footnotes to Chapter VI.

XII Journals

Journal of Indian and Buddhist Studies, since 1952. The Japanese Association for Indian Studies, c/o The Department of Indian and Buddhist Philosophy, University of Tokyo.

Monumenta Nipponica. Tokyo, Sophia University.

Young Buddhists' Bulletin. Tokyo, CIIB Press, 1959.

The Young East, since 1952. The Young East Association.

The Eastern Buddhist. Kyoto, the Eastern Buddhist Society, c/o Otani University.

The American Buddhist, since 1957. The Buddhist Churches of America, San Francisco.

Articles on special problems are mentioned in the footnotes.

E. H. NORMAN. *Andō Shōeki and the Anatomy of Japanese Feudalism.* Tokyo, The Asiatic Society of Japan, 1943.

ONO Sokyo. *The Kami Way.* (In collaboration with William P. WOODARD). International Institute for the Study of Religions, Tokyo, 1960.

KITAGAWA Joseph M. Kaiser und Schamane in Japan. *Antaios,* Band II, Nr. 6, S. 552–566.

The Three English Versions of the Kodōkwanki or Kōdokwan Record. Edited by the Meiji Japan Society, Tokyo, 1737.

KATO Genchi. *Shinto in Essence as Illustrated by the Faith in a Glorified Personality.* Tokyo, The Nogi Shrine, 1954.

KATO Genchi. *Mt. Fuji: A Glance at it by a Student of Comparative Religion.* Gotemba, the author, 1958.

FUJISAWA Chikao. *Der shintoistische Grundbegriff des Politischen und die existenzpilosophische Eigenschaft des Japanischen Kaisers.* Tokyo, Die industrielle Gesellschaft der japanischen Druckerei, 1957.

HORI Ichiro. "On the Concept of *Hijiri* (Holy-Man), *Numen.*" *International Review for the History of Religions.* International Association for the History of Religions. vol. V, fasc. 2–3, 1958, pp. 128–232.

HORI Ichiro. "Japanese Folk-Beliefs." *The American Anthropologist,* vol. 61, No. 3, June, 1959, pp. 405–424.

MIURA Baien. *Seiri Mondō.* Translated into English by Paolo BEONIO-BROCCHIERI. Published by Istituto per il Medio ed Estremo Oriente, Roma.

p. 10
p. 12
p. 16